de BONO's THINKING COURSE

Edward de Bono

British Broadcasting Corporation

Published to accompany the BBC television
series *de Bono's Thinking Course*
produced by Peter Riding
First broadcast on BBC2 from September 1982

The programmes were prepared in consultation
with the BBC Continuing Education Advisory Council

© Holland Copyright Centre B.V. 1982
First published 1982
Published by the British Broadcasting Corporation,
35 Marylebone High Street, London W1M 4AA

Text set in 11/14pt Linotron 202 Sabon, printed and bound
in Great Britain at The Pitman Press, Bath

ISBN 0 563 16500 6

Author's note

This book is more concerned with the sort of thinking that makes for wisdom rather than the sort that makes for cleverness.

If you become wise it is not so difficult to become clever as well. But if you start out by being clever you may have little chance of ever becoming wise because you can so easily get caught in the intelligence trap.

Wisdom is like a wide-angle camera lens. Cleverness is like a sharp-focus lens. In both instances someone has to hold and aim the camera. Someone has to want to take the photograph.
This book is for anyone who wants to use thinking.

Contents

Note: *How to set up a Thinking Club* is a
separate section at the end of the book,
page 157
Author's note   3

**Thinking
as a
skill**
p9

Intelligence and genes   10
Intelligence and education   10
The intelligence trap   11
Learning thinking and teaching thinking   13
The thinker   15
Self-image   16
Think slowly   17

**The
PMI**
p18

Scan   21
Interesting   22
Use of the PMI   23
Practice   24

Alternatives
p26

Easy alternatives   27
More difficult alternatives   28
The real difficulty   29
Beyond the adequate   31
The APC   33
Explanation   33
Hypothesis   34
Perception   34
Problems   34
Review   35
Design   35
Decision   36
Course of action   36
Forecasting   36
Practicality   37

Perception and patterns
p39

Perception 39
Crossing the road 44
Pattern making 45
How patterns are formed 46
The use of patterns 49
Recognition 49
Getting it wrong 50
Abstraction 51
Grouping 52
Analysis 52
Awareness 53
Art 53
Exercise 53

Lateral thinking
p55

Pattern changing 56
Humour 57
Hindsight and insight 58
Creativity and lateral thinking 59
Lateral thinking as process 60
Judgement and provocation 61
The word 'po' 63
The stepping-stone method 64
The escape method 66
The random stimulation method 68
General use of lateral thinking 70
The logic of lateral thinking 70

Information and thinking
p72

'Operacy' 73
Experience scan 74
CAF 74
C & S 75
Dense reading and dense listening 77
Logic 78
Getting more information 79
Questions 80
Experiments 81
Selecting information 82
FI-FO 82
Two uses 83

Other people p84

'Exlectics' *88*
EBS *88*
ADI *89*
Logic-bubbles *91*
OPV *93*
Constructive design *96*
Negotiation *97*
Communication *98*

Emotions and values p99

Gut feeling and thinking *99*
Emotions at three points *101*
Changing feelings *103*
Values *104*
HV and LV *104*
Value-laden words *106*
Awareness *108*

Making decisions p109

Decision pre-frame *110*
Generation of alternatives *111*
Values and priorities *111*
The dice method *111*
The easy way out method *112*
Spell-out method *113*
Balaam's ass method *113*
The ideal solution method *115*
The best home method *116*
The 'What if . . ?' method *116*
The simple matrix method *118*
The full matrix method *119*
The laziness method *120*
Decision post-frame *120*
Emphasis on fit *121*

Thinking and doing p123

'Operacy' *124*
Three ways of doing things *124*
Setting objectives *126*
AGO *126*
Targets *127*

Strategy and tactics   *128*
Courses of action   *129*
If-box maps   *130*
Planning   *132*
The terrain   *133*
People   *133*
Risks   *133*
Constraints   *133*
Resources   *134*
Future   *134*
Business and daily life   *134*

Deliberate thinking
p135

Deliberate   *135*
Focused   *135*
Confident   *136*
Enjoyable   *137*
Self-image   *137*
Time discipline   *138*
Harvesting   *139*
Thinking about thinking   *140*
The TEC framework   *141*
The 5-minute think   *142*
Symbolic TEC   *145*
PISCO   *146*
Symbolic PISCO   *146*
TEC-PISCO   *147*
Deliberate practice of thinking   *147*
Thinking clubs   *148*
General thinking skills   *148*

Summary
p151

Reference Material   *155*

How to set up a Thinking Club   *157*

Index   *167*

Thinking as a skill

There seem to be two choices.

Thinking is like walking or breathing. There is nothing we need to do about it. There is nothing we can do about it. Any interference with it will only make it awkward and artificial and inhibited by self-consciousness. If you are intelligent you are a good thinker. If you are not intelligent it is too bad and you should listen to someone who is.

Or, thinking is a skill like driving a car, juggling, cooking, skiing, playing darts or knitting. Some people will be better than others. But everyone can acquire a reasonable amount of skill if he or she wants to. That desire, or will to do it, comes first. After that comes attention, practice and enjoyment. Sometimes there seems to be more practice than enjoyment. As the skill is mastered, the fluency and effectiveness with which it is used become enjoyable. The more practice, the better things get. Perhaps thinking as a skill is more like riding a bicycle or swimming. At first there is an awkwardness and the activity seems both unnecessary and unnatural. Later it is impossible to believe that there ever was an awkward stage.

Those seem to be the two choices. If you prefer the first, then you resign yourself to your present level of thinking in the belief that there is nothing you can do to improve it. Alternatively you may be so satisfied with your present level of thinking that you cannot conceive of any further improvement. Both these attitudes seem to indicate something about the thinking used. Whether or not you believe that thinking can be improved through attention and practice, it seems worthwhile to explore that possibility because that is the only way you are going to find out whether it is just a possibility or an actual opportunity. Exploration is the best way of finding out whether exploration is worthwhile. Hope may be more appropriate than belief.

Intelligence and genes

One day we may be able to measure intelligence in a test-tube by observing certain enzyme behaviour. The extent to which intelligence is a matter of genes or early environment is much argued. It may be that an early environment satisfactory in nutrition and stimulation is needed to bring intelligence up to its full genetic potential. It may be that words, concepts and habits of mind instilled in early childhood can facilitate the operation of intelligence. It may even be that the biochemical basis of intelligence may be affected by a challenging environment. Obviously these considerations matter because they encourage us to provide as good an early environment as we can. We cannot really change our genes (technically we might be able to alter the expression of the genes with the notion, for example, that it is the aluminium in cooking pots that makes more recent generations taller than their ancestors). We can do something about early environment. We can do a great deal more about the operating skill with which intelligence is used – the skill of thinking.

Intelligence and education

It has always seemed to me that the most dangerous and obstructive fallacy in education has been the belief that intelligent people are good thinkers. Implicit in education is the notion that thinking is simply intelligence in action just as traffic is cars in motion. This fallacy is dangerous for the following two reasons.

1   If you have a high intelligence there is nothing that needs to be done about your thinking.

2   If you have a more humble intelligence there is nothing that can be done about your thinking.

The obvious result is that nothing is done to develop directly the skill of thinking. At last things are slowly beginning to change, as I shall discuss later.

It all depends on how we look at thinking and how we look at intelligence. My own definition of thinking is as follows: 'Thinking is the operating skill with which intelligence acts upon experience (for a purpose).' I have bracketed 'for a purpose' because not all thinking has a heavy sense of purpose. The definition focuses attention on three elements: operating skill, intelligence and experience.

The analogy with which I am happiest is that of a car and its driver. The car may have a powerful engine, a smooth gear box and wonderful suspension. But the skill of the driver is something different. Indeed the very power of the car may place extra demands upon that skill. In no way does the power of the car ensure the skill of the driver. In the analogy the engineering of the car corresponds to innate intelligence and the driving skill of the driver corresponds to the operating skill we call thinking. It is also often the case that a more humble car has a better driver. Driving skill can also be learned and practised and improved.

I am not especially interested in the measurement of intelligence or, indeed, of thinking skills. I prefer to be in the 'roller-skates' business. If you line up a number of people and ask them to race you will end up by comparing their natural running ability. If you design suitable roller skates for all of them they will *all* go further and faster than before. Training and coaching will also make a difference. So I am more interested in designing thinking tools and training methods than in measuring natural ability. There is nothing surprising in this. After all, the whole of mathematics is a matter of notations, concepts and techniques. We would not get very far if we relied on 'natural' mathematical ability.

The Intelligence trap

In fact it seems to be even worse than I have suggested above. Highly intelligent people may turn out to be rather poor thinkers. They may need as much, or more, training in thinking skills than other people.

This is an almost complete reversal of the notion that highly intelligent people will automatically be good thinkers. This is what we (at the Cognitive Research Trust) have come to call 'The Intelligence Trap'. There are many components to it and I shall list some of them below. Some elements are sociological, some are operational and some may even be physical.

1   A highly intelligent person can construct a rational and well-argued case for virtually any point of view. The more coherent this support for a particular point of view the less the thinker sees any need actually to explore the situation. Such a person may then become trapped into a particular view simply because he can support it.

2   Verbal fluency is often mistaken, in school and after, for thinking. An intelligent person learns this and is tempted to substitute one for the other.

3   The ego, self-image and peer status of a highly intelligent person are too often based on that intelligence. From this arises the need to be always right and clever and orthodox.

4   The critical use of intelligence is always more immediately satisfying than the constructive use. To prove someone else wrong gives you instant achievement and superiority. To agree makes you seem superfluous and a sycophant. To put forward an idea puts you at the mercy of those on whom you depend for evaluation of the idea. So too many brilliant minds are trapped into this negative mode (because it is so alluring).

5   Highly intelligent minds often seem to prefer the certainty of reactive thinking (solving puzzles, sorting data) where a mass of material is placed before them and they are asked to 'react' to it. We call this the 'Everest effect' since the existence of a tough mountain is sufficient reason for the best climbers to react to it. In projective thinking it is the thinker who has to create the context, the concepts, the objectives. The thinking has to be expansive and speculative. Through natural inclination, or perhaps early training, the highly intelligent mind seems to prefer the reactive type of thinking. Real life more usually demands the projective type.

6 The sheer physical quickness of the highly intelligent mind leads it to jump to conclusions from only a few signals. The slower mind has to wait longer and take in more signals and may reach a more appropriate conclusion.

7 The highly intelligent mind seems to prefer – or is encouraged – to place a higher value on cleverness than on wisdom. This may be because cleverness is more demonstrable. It is also less dependent on experience (which is why physicists and mathematicians often make their 'genius' contributions at an early age).

There are some other aspects of the intelligence trap. Not all highly intelligent people are caught by the intelligence trap. They may avoid it by chance, upbringing or conscious effort. The danger remains, nevertheless. And the danger cautions us not to accept the automatic assumption that high intelligence means effective thinking.

The University of Toronto School in Canada is a school for the highly gifted. It was their appreciation of this intelligence trap that lead the headmaster and some of his teachers, (in particular, Norah Maier) to start using the CoRT Thinking Lessons some years ago. My own view is that there is a tragic waste of brilliant minds when we neglect to treat thinking as a skill that can be improved by direct attention.

Learning thinking and teaching thinking

Several of the lessons in this course are derived from the *CoRT Thinking Programme*. CoRT stands for Cognitive Research Trust. The 'o' is inserted to make the abbreviation pronounceable – as in 'caught' or 'court' (and the inevitable puns).

The CoRT Thinking Lessons are now the most widely used programme in the world for the direct teaching of thinking skill as a curriculum subject in schools. They are in use in several thousand schools in the UK, Eire, Canada, Australia, New Zealand, USA, Malta and Israel (teacher training). In 1979 the newly elected Venezuelan government appointed Dr Luis Alberto Machado as

'Minister for the Development of Intelligence'. Dr Machado had read a book of mine, *The Mechanism of Mind,* which had been published in Caracas several years previously. He came to see me in England and found that the CoRT programme had already been in use for several years. The programme was translated into Spanish and adapted to local conditions. After a year's pilot study with 50 teachers who had been initially trained by me and subsequently guided by William Copley, who spent a year in Venezuela, the Minister of Education decided to put the programme into all schools. Under the direction of Dr Margaretta Sanchez 100,000 teachers have now been trained, and in the future it is intended that all youngsters (aged 10–11 years) will have 20 of the 60 CoRT lessons. There are also programmes in the technical institutes, public services and armed forces. It is a bold and courageous experiment which seems likely to be followed by other countries that appreciate that in the end 'thinking' is the ultimate human resource.

We have thirteen years of experience with the CoRT method. Exactly the same lessons are used by ten-year-olds in the middle of the Venezuelan jungle as are used by gifted students in Canada and executives in business. Sir Terence Beckett found the concepts useful when he was chairman of Ford UK. The lessons have been used over an age range of 6-year-olds (modified by Sidney Tyler) to adults, and over an ability range of IQ 75 to 150. At the present moment a Schools Council project is investigating the effects of the lessons in a group of schools where the teachers have been trained by Edna Copley.

All this is worth mentioning for several reasons. The basic thinking skills are fundamental enough to cut across age, ability and cultures. It is possible to devise simple and usable frameworks for the practice and development of thinking skills. It is possible to pay direct attention to thinking as a skill. It is possible to have these skills taught by teachers who have not had special training or (as in the case of Venezuela) where a simple form of training has been passed on through different levels of trainer. All this is important because only too often there is the comment: 'We would like to teach thinking as a skill but there is no practical way to do it.'

It is also important to realise that there is a great deal of actual experience behind the techniques put forward in this book. They are not just processes dreamed up for the sake of a television series and a book.

The methodology as described in my book, *Teaching Thinking*, is quite simple. It is based on 'tools' and 'awareness'. The tools are deliberately strange-sounding, with initials such as PMI or CAF. This is to make them tangible and usable in a deliberate fashion. They are attention directors. A person can set out to 'do a PMI'. The tools are practised on a wide range of situations. Each of these is only considered for a very short burst of time: 2 to 4 minutes. Then the thinker applies the tool to another matter. This is to ensure that attention stays on the tool rather than on the content. The big problem with teaching thinking has always been the lack of transfer. With the 'tool method' the skill is embedded in the tool. The process is neither inductive nor deductive but is 'operative'. The other element in the course is 'awareness'. This is a matter of insight, realisation, understanding of what goes on in thinking. If we get to understand the 'landscape' of thinking it becomes easier to find our way around. The tools are the means with which we get around.

The thinker

How would I define an effective thinker?

Someone who is confident of his thinking. Not confident that he is going to be right or, indeed, that he is going to find an answer to a problem: but confident that he can turn on his thinking at will and deliberately focus it in any direction he wants. Someone who is in control of his thinking instead of just drifting from idea to idea, from emotion to emotion. An effective thinker is clear about what he is setting out to do: he can define a thinking task and then set about carrying it out. He has both a clear focus and also a broad view of the situation. He favours wisdom rather than cleverness. He enjoys thinking even when it is not particularly successful. He is confident and decisive but also humble. He realises that any approach is but one amongst many – most of which he has not even thought of. He is effective and moves forward. He is robust in his thinking and practical where this is demanded. He is not content to wallow in over-intellectualisation, nit-picking or a dither of indecision. At the end of his thinking he is able to discern just what progress he has made. Even if has not reached a satisfactory answer he learns to appreciate what has been achieved – even if it is only a realisation that a great deal more thinking is required (and where to focus it).

The thinker treats thinking as a skill worth both practising and observing. He is able to think about thinking in general and his own thinking in particular. He is objective, and notes where his thinking is being less than effective. He is conscious of what needs doing even when he cannot do it. He surveys the thinking of others: not to find fault but as a map-maker might survey the terrain. He is constructive rather than critical, and supposes that the purpose of thinking is to reach a better understanding, decision or course of action: not to prove that he is smarter than someone else. He appreciates an idea just as he might appreciate a beautiful flower, no matter in whose garden it may be growing.

He treats arrogance as the major sin of thinking.

He is probably too perfect and ideal to exist. He is not unemotional. But he sees the purpose of thinking as being the arranging of experience so that his emotions can be used more fruitfully.

Self-image

Perhaps the most striking effect of the teaching of the CoRT Thinking Lessons in school is a change in self-image. Before the use of the lessons there seem to be two self-images. The first one is 'I am intelligent', which means that exams can be passed, the teacher's questions can be answered and school is a success area. The second one is 'I am not intelligent' and school is a waste of time and lessons are boring. After the CoRT lessons there is a change to a single self-image: 'I am a thinker'. This is a constructive and positive image: 'I am able to think about things, my ideas have value, I can listen to others'. The 'intelligent' or 'not-intelligent' self-images are value images which must be defended. The 'thinker' image is an operating image which is operated rather than defended. Note that the self-image of a thinker does not have to include the adjective 'good'.

Think slowly

Most of the time we think far too quickly. I include myself in that 'we'. Perhaps tests and examinations have persuaded us that there is a value in getting to the answer as quickly as possible. Yet from a thinking point of view that is wrong. Even in an emergency there is plenty of time to think slowly. In hotel fires most deaths are caused by panic. Instead of zooming through to a conclusion we need to think slowly – step by step as suggested in the Figure below. At each point we look around to see where we have got to and to explore the surroundings.

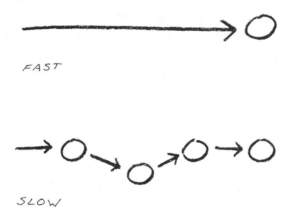

We confuse quick understanding with quick thinking and slowness with being dull-witted. If for 'slow' we substitute 'leisurely' or 'exploratory', then we can more easily appreciate the benefits of thinking more slowly.

The simple habit of trying to think more slowly can make a big difference to our effectiveness as thinkers. It is part of the general skill of thinking.

Thinking slowly means that we can focus more clearly at each stage. There are also specific focusing tools which we can use.

The PMI

I once asked seventy very bright young adults to write an essay on the suggestion that marriage be a renewable five-year contract. Sixty-seven of them wrote their opinion of the idea in the first sentence of their essay and then used the rest of the essay to support that opinion. There was no exploration of the subject other than to back up an already formed opinion. That is sometimes the style that is recommended for essay writing.

As I mentioned earlier in the book, one of the biggest faults of thinking is the use of it to back up an opinion that has already been formed (by first impression, slight thinking, prejudice or tradition). This is one of the major faults of the intelligence trap, and highly intelligent people suffer from the fault even more than others. They can so ably defend the point of view that actual exploration of the matter seems a waste of time. If you know that you are right and can demonstrate this to others, then why explore the subject?

The PMI is a powerful thinking tool that is so simple that it is almost unlearnable – because everyone thinks he or she uses it anyway. The letters are chosen to give a nicely pronounceable abbreviation so that we may ask ourselves, or others, to 'do a PMI'.

P stands for Plus or the good points

M stands for Minus or the bad points

I stands for Interesting or the interesting points

The PMI is an attention-directing tool. In doing a PMI you deliberately direct your attention first towards the Plus points, then towards the Minus points and finally towards the Interesting points. This is done in a very deliberate and disciplined manner over a period of about 2 to 3 minutes in all.

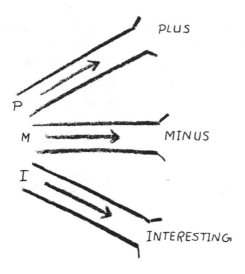

The PMI is the first of the CoRT lessons that are used in schools. The reason for putting it first is that unless some sense of the PMI is absorbed the rest of the 60 are a waste of time. The PMI sets the mood of objectivity and scanning, as I shall describe later.

I was once asked to demonstrate a CoRT lesson to a group of educators in Sydney, Australia. Before starting the lesson I asked the group of 30 boys (aged 10–11)to tell me what they thought of the idea of each of them receiving $5 a week just for going to school. All of them loved the idea and began to tell me what they would do with the money (buy sweets, comics, etc.). I then explained the PMI and asked them to go through Plus, Minus and Interesting points with regard to the $5 suggestion. They were to do this by discussion in groups of five. After three minutes a spokesman for each group gave the output. Many points were turned up:

o The bigger boys would beat them up and take the money.
o Parents would not give presents or pocket money.
o The school would raise its charges for meals.

- Who would decide how much each age level was to get?
- There would be quarrels about the money and strikes.
- Where would the money come from?
- There would be less money to pay teachers.
- There would not be any money for the school to buy a mini-bus.

At the end of the exercise the class was again asked if they liked the idea. Whereas thirty out of thirty had previously liked the idea, it now appeared that twenty-nine out of thirty had completely *reversed* their view and now disliked the idea. What is important to note is that a very simple scanning tool, used by the youngsters themselves, had brought about this change. I had made no further intervention and I had never said a word about the subject matter itself.

Suppose you were asked to do a PMI on the suggestion that all cars should be painted yellow. Your output might be something as follows:

P

- easier to see on the roads
- easier to see at night
- no problem in deciding which colour you wanted
- no waiting to get the colour you wanted
- easier for the manufacturer
- the dealer would need less stock
- it might take the 'macho' element out of car ownership
- cars would tend to become transport items
- in minor collisions the paint rubbed off on to your car is the same.

M

- boring
- difficult to recognise your car
- very difficult to find your car in a car park
- easier to steal cars
- the abundance of yellow might tire the eyes
- car chases would be difficult for the police
- accident witnesses would have a harder time
- restriction of your freedom to choose
- some paint companies might go out of business.

I

o interesting to see if different shades of yellow arose
o interesting to see if people appreciated the safety factor
o interesting to see whether attitudes towards cars changed
o interesting to see if trim acquired a different colour
o interesting to see if this were enforceable
o interesting to see who would support the suggestion.

Carrying out the process is quite easy. What is not easy is to direct attention deliberately in one direction after another when your prejudices have already decided for you what you should feel about an idea. It is this 'will' to look in a direction that is so important. Once this is achieved then the natural challenge to intelligence is to find as many P or M or I points as you can. So there is a switch. Instead of intelligence being used to support a particular prejudice it is now used to explore the subject matter.

At the end of the exploration emotions and feelings can be used to make a decision about the matter. The difference is that the emotions are now applied after the exploration instead of being applied before and so *preventing* exploration.

Scan

We sometimes call the CoRT method the 'spectacles method'. If a person is short-sighted and you give that person the appropriate spectacles then the person will be able to see more broadly and more clearly. The person's reactions will then be suited to this better view. The person can still apply exactly the same value system as was used before – but now it is applied to a better view. The thinking tools, like the PMI, perform the function of the spectacles in allowing us to see more clearly and more broadly. We then react to what we see.

One thirteen-year-old girl told how at first she thought the PMI was very artificial since she already knew what she felt about a subject. She then told how, when she had, nevertheless, put points down under P and M and I, she found herself reacting to what she had put down and her feelings changed. That is exactly what one would hope to achieve. Once an idea has been thought and put down under any of the headings, that idea cannot be 'unthought' and it will come to influence the final decision.

On one occasion one boy said that for yellow cars it would be a 'Plus' point that they would need to be kept cleaner. Another boy declared that the cleanliness was actually a 'Minus' point since he 'had to clean his Dad's car'. Both were right. The boy who saw the cleanliness point when looking in the Plus direction was correct. The boy who saw the cleanliness point when looking in the Minus direction was also correct. In the PMI we are not looking at the values that reside within the point itself. It is *not* a value judgement. We look to see what points are to be seen when we look in one direction or another. This difference is vitally important.

One girl looks towards the south and sees a church spire. Another girl in a different part of the countryside looks towards the north and sees the same church spire. Is the church a north church or a south church? Clearly it is both. It is exactly the same with the PMI. 'P' represents a scanning direction in the same way as 'north' does. We look in that direction and see what we see, we note what we see. Then we look in the next direction. The intention is solely to scan effectively – *not* to assign values.

Some people ask me whether it is in order to go through the points as they arise and then to judge each one and dump it in a category box called 'Plus' or a box called 'Minus' or another one called 'Interesting'. This is quite wrong and defeats the whole purpose of the PMI. To judge the points as they arise is a judgement exercise. To *look* in one direction after another is a scanning exercise. It is even conceivable that the chemistry of the brain is slightly different when we set out to look in a 'Plus' or positive direction from what it might be when we look in the 'Minus' or negative direction.

Because it illustrates scanning so well, the PMI is almost a miniature thinking course just by itself.

Interesting

The 'I' or Interesting element of the PMI has several functions. It can collect all those points and comments which are neither positive nor negative. (It might be noted that if a particular point is seen both in the **P** and also in the **M** direction it is quite in order to include it under both headings.) The **I** also encourages the deliberate habit of exploring a matter outside of the judgement framework to see what is interesting about the idea or what it leads to. A simple phrase which is useful for carrying through this I scan is: 'It would be interesting to see if . . .' The thinker is thereby encouraged to expand the idea rather than just to treat it as static.

Another aspect of the 'I' direction is to see if the idea leads to another idea. This notion of the 'movement value' of an idea will be explored much more fully in the lateral thinking section of this book.

Finally the 'I' trains the mind to react to the interest inherent in an idea and not just to judgement feelings about the idea. A thinker should be able to say: 'I do not like your idea but there are these interesting aspects to it . . . .' It is a common enough experience that this sort of reaction is highly unusual.

Use of the PMI

Many people would claim to do the PMI anyway. This is possibly true for those situations about which there is a great deal of indecision. But that is not the main purpose of the PMI. On the contrary, the PMI should most especially be used when we have *no doubt* about the situation but have instantly decided that we like it or do not like it (like the Sydney schoolboys' reaction to the $5 a week). As a habit of mind the PMI is specifically designed to force us to scan in those situations where otherwise we should deem scanning unnecessary.

For example, you can ask someone to 'do a PMI' when that person has summarily dismissed your suggestion as valueless. You can ask someone to 'do a PMI' when there seems to be a prejudged reaction to a situation. The PMI is useful because it is more oblique than direct disagreement or confrontation. In the PMI you are asking the person to exhibit his or her great intelligence in doing a scan of the subject. This is totally different from asking a person to reverse an opinion. Normally the person so asked is not afraid to do a PMI because he or she feels that this will only support the view that is already held.

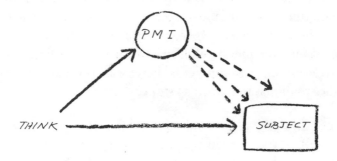

I once carried out an experiment with 140 senior executives. I divided them into two random groups according to the date of each person's birthday (odd or even). I then gave each group a suggestion to consider and decide upon. One group got the suggestion of 'a dated currency so that each year the currency would have the year on it and there might be exchange rates between these different dates'. The other group were asked to consider 'that marriage be a five-year renewable contract'. The initial decisions were collected. The problems were now switched. This time the PMI was explained and each person was asked to do a PMI before making a decision. If everyone had been doing something of the sort in the first place no change would be expected (assuming the groups were random). But there was change. Before the PMI 44% were in favour of the dated currency, but after the PMI only 11% were in favour. The opposite happened with the contract marriage suggestion: before the PMI 23% were in favour, but after the PMI this rose to 38%.

Doing a PMI is not really the same as listing the 'pros and cons' which tends to be more of a judgement exercise. In addition the 'Interest' direction allows consideration of those matters which would not fall under either pro or con.

Practice

Because the PMI seems so very simple its effectiveness should not be underestimated. I have seen it used to turn a fiercely emotional meeting from prejudice towards consideration of the subject. Once perception is directed in a certain direction it cannot help but see, and once seen something cannot be unseen.

The key is practice. Practise doing the PMI yourself and practise demanding it of others. It can become a simple shorthand instruction. The strangeness of the lettering is important in order to give focus. Mere exhortation to someone to look at the good points and bad points is much too weak to be effective.

For practice a PMI can be done on each of the three practice items listed here. Three minutes should be allowed for the whole PMI in each case. The items can be done on one's own or in a small discussion group.

1   What do you think of the suggestion that everyone should wear a badge showing his or her mood?
2   Should every child adopt an old person to look after?
3   Are weekend prisons for young offenders a good idea?

Alternatives

The natural tendency of thinking is to support a view arrived at by other means. That is what makes the PMI so important a tool: it counteracts this natural tendency. In an exactly parallel manner, the deliberate search for alternatives is an extremely important part of the skill of thinking because this also counteracts the natural tendency of mind. The natural tendency of mind is towards certainty, security and arrogance. This arises from the way in which it works as a pattern-making and pattern-using system which I shall be describing in the next section. The mind wants to recognise and identify with certainty as soon as possible. Certainty of recognition means that action can be taken. A clutch of alternatives means that no action can yet be taken since it is difficult to move in several directions at once – and impossible if some of the directions are contradictory. Alternatives also suggest dither.

A good doctor wants to diagnose the illness and get on with the treatment. This doctor metaphor illustrates the dilemma. As a patient, which would you prefer:– a doctor who rushed in, came to a rapid diagnosis based on his considerable experience, insisted arrogantly on that diagnosis and treated you with immense confidence; or a doctor who examined you carefully, generated as many possible alternatives as he could, checked these out with tests, finally came to a diagnosis and treated you accordingly (still keeping his mind open to a change in diagnosis). In practise you might actually prefer the first doctor with his great confidence. You certainly would not want the second doctor to tell *you* all the possible alternatives and you would not want him to be tentative or dithering. Intellectually you would appreciate, however, that the great confidence of the first doctor would equally apply when he was making a terrible mistake.

The mind tends to work like the first doctor because we have to get on with life and a flurry of alternatives too often means a dither of indecision.

Because of this natural tendency of mind we need to develop a conscious tool. As with the PMI we want to provide ourselves with a concrete instruction which we can then use with ourselves and with others whenever it seems that a search for alternatives is required. The tool is the APC (A is for Alternatives; P is for Possibilities; C is for Choices). We shall be looking at the practical use of this tool later in this section.

Easy alternatives

Sometimes it is easy and fun to look for alternatives. We get a certain enjoyment out of each new alternative we can turn up. The drawing below does not represent anything in particular. The task is to list all the different things it might represent. You can put down the book at this stage and generate as many alternatives as you can. Or, you can read the suggestions listed here and then try to add further ones of your own.

o two helium filled balloons
o doughnuts on sticks
o polo mints on sticks
o flowers
o trees
o target (for cross-eyed gentlemen)

- end view of two long tubes
- dead roller skate
- overhead view of two cooks frying eggs on a verandah
- overhead view of two Mexicans doing something against a wall
  and so on . . .

The task is fun and not particularly difficult. It is, however, difficult to get *all* the possibilities. Very often an alternative which seems very obvious in hindsight is extremely elusive – until someone else suggests it.

Imagine a glass full of water standing on a table. The task is to empty the glass of water. You are not allowed to damage the glass in any way or to tilt it. How many different approaches can you think of? As before you can put the book aside and list these approaches or you can read further and then add further alternatives of your own.

- siphon or suck water out
- blow water out
- use detergent and bubble water out
- capillary action (as with a rag)
- boil water away
- freeze water and lift out
- centrifuge glass
- put sand, pebbles or object in glass to displace water
- use sponge or absorbent material
- use water-filled balloon to displace the water and then lift out and
  so on . . .

Once again this task is relatively easy because there are few constraints (as to practicality, cost, mess etc.).

More difficult alternatives

Many years ago I was sitting next to the famous mathematician, Professor Littlewood, at dinner in Trinity College. We were talking about getting computers to play chess. We agreed that chess was difficult because of the large number of pieces and the different moves. It seemed an interesting challenge to design a game that was as simple as possible and yet could be played with a degree of skill. As a result of that challenge I designed the 'L-Game', in which each player has only one piece (the L-shape piece). In turn he moves this to any new vacant position (lifting up, turning over, moving across the board to a vacant position, etc.). After moving his L-piece he can – if he wishes – move either one of the small neutral pieces (shown as a circle in the diagram) to any new position. The object of the game is to block your opponent's L-piece so that no move is open to it.

The game is shown in the drawing below. The starting position is shown. How many alternative moves are open to the player who starts first? I make it 60, but that also includes movements of the neutral pieces. Even the alternative moves of the L-piece are not immediately obvious to someone who does not know the game.

(c) de Bono 1969, UK patent 1148172

Another task. In how many different ways could you divide a square into four equal pieces so that each piece was of the same size, shape and area? In practice most people can rattle through about six or seven different ways. There are, in fact, an infinite number of ways of dividing up a square in this manner. There are also several alternative ways of creating this infinite variety of shapes. In this case some of the approaches are not so easy to find – yet all of them are obvious in hindsight.

The real difficulty

When we actually set out to find alternatives it is not all that difficult to find some (it may be difficult to find many and almost impossible to find all of them). The real difficulty is to set out to look for alternatives in the first place.

Some time ago I had to catch an early morning flight from Los Angeles to Toronto and so I set the alarm clock in my hotel bedroom to go off at 4.30 am. It was one of those radio-type alarm clocks. At 4.30 am the alarm went off. Mindful of my neighbours and the early hour I pressed the snooze button which is supposed to allow a few more minutes of sleep. Nothing happened. I pressed the 'off' switch. Nothing happened. I set the alarm to radio instead of buzzer. Nothing happened. I tried to re-set the alarm time. Nothing happened. I pulled the plug out of the wall. Nothing happened (this is not so surprising since many such clocks contain batteries to tide them over short power failures). I put a pillow over the clock. Nothing happened. At this point I seemed to have two choices: I could call the reception desk and feebly enquire how I might silence my clock; or I could throw the thing in a bucket of water. It was only then – and by chance – that I noticed that the loud buzzing noise was not coming from the radio clock at all but from my other small clock which I had set and forgotten about.

The moral of the story is that at no point did I pause even to consider whether there could be an alternative source of the noise. It seemed so obvious to me that it *must* be the radio clock that I had set, that I never set out to look for alternatives. Had I done so I could have saved myself a great deal of trouble. And all this was happening to someone who from time to time considers himself creative.

There is a counterbalancing story. At a seminar of mine in Australia a senior computer man seemed to be having a hard time appreciating the purpose of lateral thinking. After the coffee break on the second day he came to me with more enthusiasm. What he said was this: 'For twenty-five years I have been putting two packets of sugar in my coffee. I have always opened one packet and then the other. Today, without apparently thinking about it, I found myself placing one packet on top of the other and making one opening operation. Much simpler.'

In both those stories the difficulty was not in finding an alternative but in ever *setting out* to look for one.

Beyond the adequate

There is a simple experiment which has worked for me every time I have tried it. I used it again in the BBC Television series 'de Bono's Thinking Course'. Two small boards are placed on the floor. Each has a hole in the end. On each board is a coiled piece of string. The task is to use the boards to cross the floor of the room in such a manner that no part of the body or clothing comes into contact with the ground. The task was given to a young lad.

Sometimes the thinker stands on one board and pushes out the other board ahead of him, moves to that board, retrieves the first board and pushes that further ahead. This sort of stepping-stones approach works but is slow.

A more usual response is to use the string to tie one board to each foot and then to shuffle across the room as if on skis or snow-shoes.

A rather better approach – which I have never seen used spontaneously – is to forget about one of the boards. The string is tied to the front of the remaining board. The thinker steps on to that board, uses the string to hold the board up against the soles of his feet, and hops across the room at a great rate.

The 'shuffle' solution seems so obvious and so adequate that there never seems any need to set out to look for an alternative.

Contentment with an 'adequate' solution or approach is the biggest block there is to any search for a better alternative.

In a previous book, *Practical thinking*, I coined the phrase 'Village Venus effect'. The inhabitants of a remote village (pre-TV days) know that the most beautiful girl in the village is the most beautiful girl in the world. They have no way of conceiving that there can be anyone more beautiful until after they have experienced that additional beauty. So it often is in science, in industry, in government and in other areas. We are very happy with what we have because we cannot conceive of anything better – and until we can conceive of something better we are not motivated to look for it. It is only through realisation of this and an act of *will* that we can set out to look for alternatives – knowing that in most cases we shall not find anything better, but still being willing to invest that thinking time.

In that same book I put forward what I called 'de Bono's second law'. This states quite simply that:

'Proof may be no more than lack of imagination.'

Often we are convinced of an hypothesis or explanation simply because we cannot imagine an alternative explanation. A classic example of this is Darwin's theory of evolution. It is plausible and rational and better than anything else. It is also impossible to prove. Our proof for it rests on our lack of imagination in thinking of a better mechanism. Similarly, we reject Lamarckian evolution because we cannot conceive how it could occur. Part of Darwin's theory is a tautology: if something survives it must be a survivor. As to the mechanism of change, that could well happen in viruses or bacteria which go through generations several thousand times faster than animals. The change is then transferred to the animal by genetic transference which we know can take place. Or we might even have non-genetic evolution with chemical inducers and suppressors passed from mother to child in unbroken continuity (this could lead to Lamarckianism).

On the whole, adequate theories in science are the biggest block to progress. But to open the floodgates to all sorts of wild and woolly theories would be quite impractical.

In practice in science, we stay with one hypothesis until we can reject it. Then we move on to a better one. In order to reject the hypothesis we carry out experiments with which we actually hope to confirm it (such is human nature and human ego needs). The fallacy with this approach is that the existing hypothesis determines our perceptions and the sort of evidence that we look for. Thus it often needs mistake, accident or chance to provide the instrusive evidence we could never have looked for when holding the orthodox hypothesis. So what should we do about it? The simple answer is to change the idiom. Instead of just holding the best hypothesis we spend a lot of time generating alternative ones – not in order to reject them in favour of the best one but in order to allow us to look at things more broadly. But scientists, like many others, have never been particularly concerned with the operations of thinking.

The APC

As I mentioned earlier APC stands for Alternatives, Possibilities and Choices. The three words are there in order to make APC pronounceable. In different situations one or other word may seem more appropriate but no attempt should be made to distinguish between them. Doing an APC means making a deliberate effort to generate alternatives at that particular point.

As with the PMI, the APC does no more than actualise the desire to look for alternatives 'at this particular point'. There is no magic about it and at the same time there is a lot of effectiveness in it. It converts a general desire into a specific operating instruction (or 'executive concept').

We can look now at some of the situations in which we may want to 'do an APC'.

Explanation

A young man is seen to be pouring cans of beer into the petrol tank of his car at a petrol station. Do an APC on this. What possible explanations might there be for this behaviour? Some starting alternatives are given below: add to them.

- o it was not his car: he was sabotaging it
- o he was drunk
- o it was an advertising stunt for beer
- o it was petrol but the pump was out of action so he used cans and so on . . . .

In judging the behaviour of others, in trying to explain a swing in a political poll and in examining market behaviour, we need to create alternative explanations no matter how likely one of them may seem. The search is not for the most likely but for the most likely *and* a number of others as well. Explanation is an area where it is only too easy to be trapped by the adequate.

Hypothesis

Although men seem to be smoking less, women seem to be smoking more. Do an APC on this and put forward some alternative hypotheses as to why this might be. There are times when an hypothesis is virtually the same as an explanation. On the whole an explanation refers to a single happening or instance, whereas hypothesis refers to some process or trend. As I mentioned earlier, we need to generate alternative hypotheses no matter how tempted we are to consider one of them the best and 'true' one.

Perception

In New Zealand I was once talking to a group of senior industrialists about opportunity development. Many of them complained that in New Zealand there were so many restrictions and regulations that it was difficult to pursue opportunities. One of them looked at things in an alternative way. He welcomed the regulations by saying: 'If you learn how to cope with the regulations just think how effectively they keep back your competitors, and new entrants, who cannot cope – so I see them as enhancing opportunity.'

A research project was condemned for wasting money when it set out to show that in schools with swimming pools the children spent more time swimming. Do an APC on this: how else could you look at the project?

Problems

With problems, an APC can be done at several points. This first is in the definition of the problem. The best definition of a problem can only be reached by finding the solution and then working backwards to the definition. But we can look for alternative definitions of the problem. Do an APC on alternative definitions of the peak travel problem in city transport.

When it comes to tackling the problem we can generate a number of different approaches instead of just searching for the best one from the start. Do an APC on approaches to the peak travel problem in cities: try to generate about four different approaches.

Finally, when we have an adequate solution to a problem, we can go beyond the adequate and search for different solutions. The satisfaction of finding a solution at all makes us very unwilling to look for another one. Besides, the other solution may be found by someone else!

Review

A problem is something we are forced to tackle. In a review we need to make an effort of will to look again at something which is not a problem, which is going reasonably well, which does not demand attention. We look at it, however, to see if the process could be simplified or made more effective or more productive. This always involves seeing if there are other ways of carrying out the operation (and also whether it needs to be done at all). Do an APC (review style) on the packaging of chocolate bars.

Design

In design we set out to create something that is going to achieve some purpose. In a sense it is much freer than problem-solving because, provided we achieve the purpose, we can use different approaches and different styles.

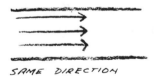

SAME DIRECTION

The important point here – as far as APC goes – is to realise when you are using alternatives which lie within the same general approach and when you really are using a totally different approach. Only too often, in my experience, a proposed alternative approach is only an alternative within the same basic approach.

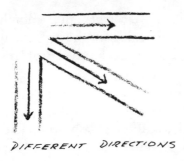

DIFFERENT DIRECTIONS

Do an APC on the design of a telephone.

Decision

Business schools and management training put a great deal of emphasis on making decisions – as I shall do later in this book. It is assumed that the alternatives are obvious and easy to find. Yet very often, difficulty in making a decision stems from a failure to produce sufficient alternatives. The decision process itself will not produce these alternatives. We need to shift some emphasis away from the deciding between alternatives to the generating of alternatives. A competitor undercuts the price of the toilet rolls your company is selling. You are asked to decide whether you should lower prices to match his. Do an APC on the alternatives available for your decision.

Course of action

I am told that there is an old Jewish saying which states that if there are two courses of action you should always take the third. As in decision making, this properly shifts the emphasis to the search for alternatives. Finding courses of action involves problem solving, design and decision making. Do an APC on the courses of action open to you if you invented a new children's game.

Forecasting

In business as in many other areas it is important to try to tell something about the future. Decisions and plans made now are going to operate in the future. Investments made now are going to pay off in the future. All future forecasting is based on the extrapolation of present trends. No matter how incorrect this method may be, there is no way anyone would ever be brought to believe in a forecast derived in any other way. Yet we know there will be discontinuities and the future will not just consist of present trends carried forwards. The best we can do is to generate alternative futures in a deliberate manner and allow them to enrich our perception even though we will never believe them until after they have happened. Science fiction performs a useful function in this respect. Do an APC on possible future scenarios for the entertainment industry.

The above list of situations in which an APC might be useful is not complete. We should also look at negotiation, communication, opportunity search, investment, planning and many other areas. What matters is being able to say to ourselves, or others in the group, 'let's do an APC at this point'.

Practicality

There are two common objections to the APC process. The first is that it is a waste of time and creates unnecessary work. The second is that too many alternatives create a dither of indecision. Both have some validity.

The answer to the first objection is that there is no way of telling that the first answer to a problem is the best one until at least some effort has been made to find other answers. Further alternatives in a decision situation do increase the work of deciding between them . That is just too bad. You can never improve your decision by impoverishing the range of alternatives. Anyone who does not like the work of decision making should get out of that job.

The answer to the second objection is to be ruthless about practical cut-offs. Sir Robert Watson-Watt, the father of radar, apparently had a saying: 'You get one idea today, you get a better idea tomorrow, you get the best idea . . . never.' With that I agree. The designer who is forever changing the design makes production impossible. If I were to re-write my manuscripts they would always get better — but never get published as the process of improvement can be never ending.

So there is a need for practical cut-offs and deadlines and the freezing of designs.

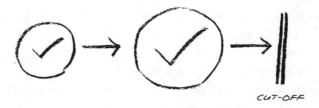

CUT-OFF

The main point is that we should not be reluctant to look for alternatives because we cannot conceive of anything better than what we have. The secondary point is that we should not be afraid to look for alternatives for fear of the extra hassle they might cause.

Perception and patterns

What is the main purpose of thinking?

The main purpose of thinking is to abolish thinking. The mind works to make sense out of confusion and uncertainty. The mind works to recognise in the outside world familiar patterns. As soon as such a pattern is recognised the mind switches into it and follows it along – further thinking is unnecessary. It is not unlike driving a car. As soon as you hit a familiar road you can stop figuring it out from the map, using a compass, asking for directions or even reading road signs. In a way, our thinking is a continuing search for these familiar roads that make thinking unnecessary.

But how are these patterns formed and how does the mind use them? How does it affect our thinking and what should we do about it?

In order to understand thinking we need to know something about how the mind works as an information processing system. This is what I intend to deal with in this section.

This section is an 'awareness' section. The PMI and the APC were tools that could be practised and used. I hope in this section to illustrate some aspects of how the mind works. Such an awareness is an important part of general thinking skill.

Perception

In my book *The Mechanism of Mind* I told the following story.

On my first day at Oxford I was going off to a party in London. The college gates were closed at midnight and I knew that I would be back late. So I asked one of the old hands about climbing back into college. He indicated that it was quite simple. There was one wall to be climbed and then a second wall and then you jumped down from the top of the bicycle shed into the quadrangle. I returned at about three in the morning and proceeded to climb the first wall which was about fifteen feet in height. I dropped down on the other side and proceeded until I came to the second wall, which was the same height. I climbed the second wall and dropped down on the other side. It took quite a while to dawn on me that I was out in the meadow again: I had climbed in and out across a corner as shown in the drawing below. I started all over again. This time I was more careful in exploring the second wall. I found an iron gate, which offered easier footholds. I climbed to the top of the gate which then swung slowly open: it had never been closed. Eventually I got in.

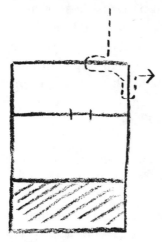

I was telling that story to a computer group when someone at the meeting said that he had had a similar experience at the same place. It seemed, however, that he had had somewhat more to drink. He climbed to the top of the wall, lost his balance and fell off. This did not worry him too much. He got to his feet and proceeded to climb over the wall. Unfortunately he had fallen off on the *inside*. So he found that he had indeed climbed out into the meadow.

The moral of the two stories is very clear: excellence in wall climbing does not itself ensure that the right wall is being climbed. That moral is profoundly important for thinking. For 'wall-climbing' read 'processing', for 'wall identification' read 'perception'. So we find that excellence in processing does not make up for inadequacies of perception.

Perception is the way we look at things. Processing is what we do with that perception. In our thinking we have accepted three fallacies. The first is that it does not matter where you start (ie your perception) because if your thinking is good enough you will reach the right answer. The second is that from within the situation, through the use of further processing, you can tell where you ought to have started. The third is that the traditional perception is sufficient because it has evolved through trial and error over time. These three fallacies have made us concern ourselves with processing, for which we have developed such marvellous tools as mathematics. We have neglected the perception area because there did not seem to be much we could do about it.

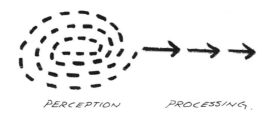

PERCEPTION   PROCESSING.

The paradox is that it is the development of the computer with its superb 'processing' capabilities that has shifted attention back to the perception area. Once we can take processing for granted then perception becomes even more important, because the way we look at a situation will determine what we can do about it.

In practical life most thinking takes place in the perception area: how we get to look at things. It is only in rather specialised situations that we then have to proceed to elaborate processing. In the future we shall be able to delegate more and more processing to computers. That leaves the perceptual sort of thinking to humans. And we need to get very much better at it.

My favourite illustration of the problem of perception is the oil and vinegar problem (which I have used elsewhere as the wine and water problem). You are about to make a salad dressing and have before you a glass of olive oil and a glass of wine vinegar. You take a spoonful of oil from the oil glass and pour it into the vinegar glass. You stir thoroughly and then take a spoonful of the mixture and put it back in the oil glass. You stop at this point. Is there now more oil in the vinegar or vinegar in the oil, or what? (It does not matter but we can suppose the spoon to be less than one-fifth the volume of the glass.)

I wrote in an earlier book, *The Use of Lateral Thinking*, that it seemed to me there would be as much oil in the vinegar glass as vinegar in the oil glass. My publishers were highly sceptical of this assertion. After publication a logician wrote politely to point out my error. He said that the spoonful of oil was a spoonful of pure oil. The return spoonful was a spoonful of mixture and hence contained less vinegar than the first spoon had contained oil. So there should be more oil in the vinegar than vinegar in the oil. The logic seems impeccable. But the perception is faulty.

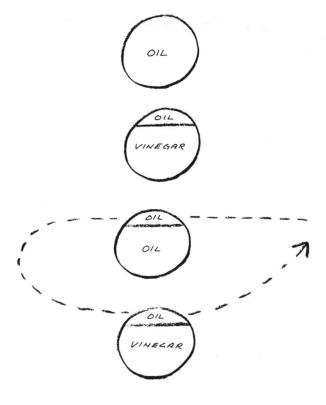

A different way of looking at the matter is shown above. The two spoonfuls are of equal volume. The first spoonful contains pure oil. The second spoonful contains a mixture, which is shown by letting the oil float on top of the vinegar. But where has this small amount of oil come from? Obviously from the vinegar glass. But that glass contained no oil in the beginning. So the little bit of oil must have done a round trip: travelling across in the first spoonful and back in the second. It ends up where it started, so we can forget about it. If we now subtract this same amount of oil from both spoonfuls we must be left with equal volumes in each: in one case a volume of oil and in the other a volume of vinegar. So the exchange of oil and vinegar must be equal. It matters not at all how much oil comes back. In fact it does not even matter if the oil is never stirred into the vinegar glass.

If you start adding the odd number beginning at 1 you will always get a square:

$1 + 3 = 4 = 2^2$

$1 + 3 + 5 = 9 = 3^2$

$1 + 3 + 5 + 7 = 16 = 4^2$

How might you set about proving that this must always be so? There are many possible approaches to this problem. A particularly easy approach is shown below.

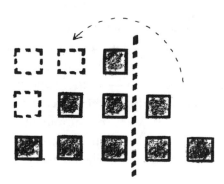

The numbers are looked upon as stacked boxes. If we added up all the rows we would have $1 + 3 + 5 + 7 \ldots$ If we made the stack higher we would really be adding the next odd number. All we now have to do is to cut a piece of the stack off and show how it fits round on the other side — so giving a square. This will always hold no matter how high the stack may be.

Both the above examples are intended to illustrate the difference between perception and processing. Perception is how we look at things in the first place. Processing is what we do with that perception.

Crossing the road

The drawing below shows a noughts-and-crosses grid. If you start in any square and then proceed to any other square and then on to any further square (and so on until all squares have been visited once), in how many different ways could you make the journey? Some people say 27 and some say several hundred. The right number (I think) is no less than 362,880. This unexpectedly large number simply reflects the large numbers that occur in the mathematics of combination (the number of ways in which different things can be put together).

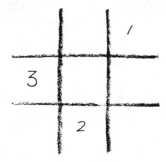

I once invented a simple jig-saw which had but 16 pieces that were all square. The task was to arrange these 16 pieces to form a large square of a certain design. But the design did not emerge until all the pieces had been placed in the right position — so there was no way of telling which piece ought to fit against which other piece. Each small square had two faces: upper and lower. With this simple jig-saw of just 16 pieces it would take many million years to go through all the possible combinations — even if one piece was placed every second, day and night.

If we had to cross a road by analysing all the information coming to us and trying it out in different ways it would take us more than a month just to get across.

We do not take a month to cross the road because the mind does not work in that way. We cross the road in a suitable time because the mind is designed to be 'brilliantly uncreative'. If the mind was anything else it would be quite useless.

Pattern making

The mind (in perception) provides a means whereby incoming information gets organised into a pattern – as suggested in the drawing below. We shall see shortly how this actually comes about.

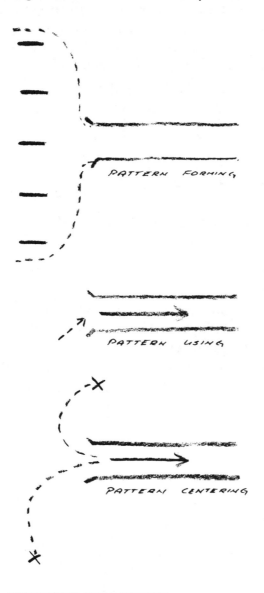

PATTERN FORMING

PATTERN USING

PATTERN CENTERING

Once a pattern has been formed then the mind no longer has
to analyse or sort information. All that is required is enough
information to trigger the pattern. The mind then follows along the
pattern automatically in the same way as a driver follows a familiar
road. So any vague movement along the road at a certain speed is
instantly treated as an approaching vehicle.

There is another important characteristic of the patterning system
of the mind. Unless there are competing patterns, then anything
remotely similar to the established pattern will be treated just as if it
were that pattern. It is not unlike the watershed into a valley. Unless
there is a competing valley, water which falls quite far away will end
up at the centre of the valley. This is what we might call 'the
centering of patterns'. This is suggested below.

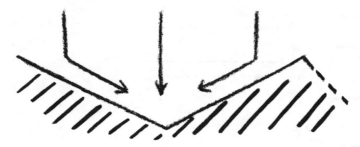

How patterns are formed

A tray of sand is shown below. A steel ball is dropped on to the
surface of the sand at a specific point. The ball sinks into the sand
and remains exactly at the point at which it was dropped. This is the
same as making a pencil mark on a piece of paper at a certain point
or changing the magnetism of a magnetic tape at a certain point. The
paper, the tape and the sand all carry a passive and accurate record of
what has happened to them. All our information recording systems
are of this passive type.

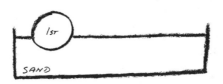

We also have a tray into which is inserted a moulded plastic surface. Again we drop a steel ball on to the surface, just as we did for the sand. This time the ball does not stay where it has been dropped but rolls along until it reaches the bottom of the dip. No matter from where we dropped the ball it would always end up in this same position. This surface is now 'altering' the information that is coming in. Unlike the sand tray, the plastic tray does not keep an accurate record of what has happened to it. The incoming information is altered or 'curved'. This is no longer a passive information system but an active one.

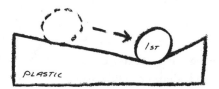

We pass to the third tray in the drawing below. This contains a heavy viscous fluid covered by a stout membrane. A steel ball is dropped on to the surface. Gradually it sinks in. When it comes to rest the membrane is depressed to give an appearance similar to that in the plastic tray. If a further steel ball is dropped on the surface it will roll down the slope and end up nestling against the first ball. Like the plastic surface tray, this 'viscous' tray is an active information system. In the plastic tray the contours were formed before the first ball arrived. In the viscous tray it is the first ball, itself, which forms the contours. In fact the viscous tray is an environment in which incoming information can organise itself into clusters.

We can now move to another model. This time the passive surface is a towel laid on a table. There is a bowl of ink alongside. A spoonful of ink is taken from the bowl and poured on to the towel at some specific spot. The ink leaves a stain at that spot. The process is repeated to give the final arrangement as shown overleaf. The towel surface is an accurate and passive memory surface.

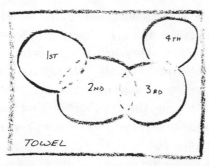

TOWEL

Instead of the towel we now have a shallow dish of gelatine or jelly. The bowl of ink is heated up. When a spoonful of hot ink is placed on the gelatine surface it dissolves the gelatine. When the cooled ink and dissolved gelatine are poured off, a shallow depression remains on the surface of the gelatine. If a further spoonful is placed on the surface in the same position, as was done with the towel, then the hot ink will flow into the depression making it deeper. The same thing will happen with the third and fourth spoonfuls. In the end a sort of 'channel' or 'track' will have been eroded in the surface of the gelatine, as illustrated below. There is a close similarity between the gelatine surface and the viscous tray. In both cases the first arriving information altered the surface. This altered surface then affected the way in which further information was received. The gelatine model is more sophisticated because the information essentially 'organises itself into a track or pattern'.

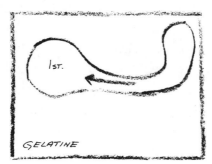

GELATINE

Once the pattern has been formed then any information that reaches that pattern or channel will 'flow' along it – always in the same way and establishing the pattern ever more definitely.

The viscous tray and the gelatine dish illustrate how certain types of surface can provide an environment in which incoming information may organise itself into patterns. The nerve networks in the mind seem to work in a somewhat similar manner. How these interconnected nerve networks allow incoming information to organise itself into patterns is described in detail in another book of mine: *The Mechanism of Mind*. Those who want this further detail should read that book.

At this point it is enough to appreciate how 'active' information systems are different from our usual 'passive' systems. How such systems allow information to organise itself into patterns.

We can now forget all about how the patterns come to be formed and treat them as channels, roads or tracks. Once you enter at the beginning you move or 'flow' along to the end.

The use of patterns

The purpose of perception is to allow patterns to form and then to use them. As suggested earlier, the purpose of thinking is to find the familiar pattern and so remove the need to think any more. We can look at this use of patterns under a number of headings.

Recognition

When you are reading poor handwriting it may take a while to recognise a word. Then suddenly it becomes clear. With print we recognise the words so rapidly that we are hardly aware of this 'pattern recognition'. It is only when there is any difficulty (for example, recognising a familiar voice over a bad telephone connection) that we become aware of the active process of recognition: the effort to identify the pattern.

Adults often take hours or days to work out the Rubik's cube puzzle. Children can do it in minutes and the record is in the region of 25 seconds. Clearly this does not give much time for working things out. Pattern recognition is used. The recognition of a certain pattern triggers a course of action which in turn leads to another pattern, which triggers another course of action and so on to the end.

This pattern recognition is a most marvellous property of the human mind. It allows us to greet friends and to use languages. It allows us to eat and to live. The whole of conscious life is based upon it. In perception the entire effort is directed towards recognising familiar patterns.

Getting it wrong

The drawing below shows a design for a rather special wooden cube. Someone has given this design to a carpenter and asked him to construct the cube. The upper half is going to be made of one type of wood and the lower half of another type. The two halves are to be joined by proper dovetail joints as shown. The cube design looks exactly the same from the other side. The question is whether it would be possible for the carpenter actually to make up the cube.

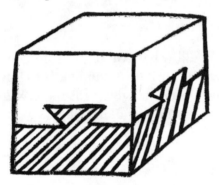

At first sight it would seem to be impossible. We imagine that the joint lines would run as shown below. It would be impossible to put the pieces together or to separate them if they had somehow been assembled. Using this pattern we should reject the design.

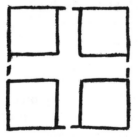

But the pattern is a wrong one. It is possible to make up the cube. It is also possible to separate the top half from the bottom half after the cube has been assembled. The usual pattern is to expect the joint lines to run at right angles as shown earlier. Instead they run at an angle as shown here. As a result the top half is easily slid on to or off from the lower half.

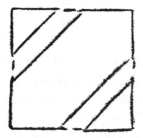

In this instance pattern recognition has led us astray because we have recognised the wrong pattern. It is inevitable that in a pattern-recognising system we should use the wrong pattern from time to time. It also follows that the fewer the patterns we have the more often are we going to use the wrong ones.

Abstraction

The mind is good at recognising whole patterns, such as faces, letters or words. It is also extremely good at abstracting or pulling out hidden patterns. If you take eight random objects and put their names down as a list there is a very high likelihood that an observer would be able to divide those words into two groups of four by abstracting some pattern. Yet the words were chosen at random. Consider the list below.

dog
umbrella
fish
car
toothpaste
desk
hat
money

In how many ways could you divide that list into two groups of four? You can try this exercise with any eight random words. If you do it with an audience you may be surprised at the variety of patterns that are abstracted.

Are the abstracted patterns in the material or in the way we choose to look at it? They are triggered by the material and finally are checked against the material, but the patterns have to exist in our mind before we can use them.

Grouping

The process of grouping makes life very much easier. Instead of having to learn about every single car, we can group them all into the general group of 'cars' and for some purposes (like crossing the road), treat them all as similar. Grouping and classification also allows us to make certain predictions about things. We identify something as belonging to a group (for example, a vehicle as belonging to the 'car' group), and then we go on to infer that the object also possesses the properties of the group (that the vehicle has a steering wheel). This was the basis of classical philosophy. All we are really saying is that we expect certain clusters of properties to go together so that if we identify some properties we can predict the rest by using the established pattern.

'Lumpers' are those people who tend to group things together by focusing on common features. 'Splitters' are those people who tend to separate things out by focusing on points of difference. Science is based on a judicious mix of lumping and splitting.

Analysis

There are really two sorts of analysis. In the first sort we strive to break down a complex situation into familiar and recognisable patterns. We suppose that these elements have actually come together to produce the situation: they are components. The second type of analysis is more like explanation. We look to see what familiar patterns we can recognise in the situation but never suppose that they are the actual components of the situation. This last sort is very close to abstraction.

Chinese science was quite far advanced long before science developed in the West. Then the theorists got to work and created all sorts of explanations: layers of different spirits and hobgoblins which made things happen in certain ways. Science died. This was the explanation type of analysis. Western science has tried to follow the 'component' type of analysis and has eschewed the hobgoblin approach. The dilemma is that too many concepts stagnate a subject (because everything is possible) and too few concepts stagnate a subject (because evidence is led by concepts).

Awareness

We need to be aware of the huge importance of the perception part of thinking.

We need to be aware that in perception the mind works as a self-organising information system (active system) which allows incoming experience to organise itself into patterns. This is a marvellous system which allows us to make sense of the world. Without it life would be impossible.

We need to be aware that the purpose of thinking is to search for these familiar patterns and then to stop thinking as we race along them.

We need to be aware that we may often lock into the wrong pattern.

We need to be very much aware that the repertoire of patterns which we have in our minds will determine our recognition, our abstraction, our classifications, our analysis and all our thinking.

Art

One of the purposes of art is to help us stock our mind with further patterns. Art crystallises patterns of experience so that we can absorb them without having had to live through and learn them by a slow process of induction. Art can also give us a range of experience we would never otherwise have had. In a sense art is an accelerated life machine.

Exercise

It is a useful habit to stand back and then to try to pick out the patterns that seem to be in use in certain situations. For instance, in much psychotherapy the pattern is still Freudian: dig deep and find what unconscious explanations there are for feelings and behaviour. In education the pattern is that it is enough to provide information and then allow the mind to acquire thinking habits as it deals with that information. In politics it is the adversary system in which opposing parties claim the rightness of their ideologies and seek electoral permission to impose that ideology on everyone.

As an exercise, try to pick out the basic patterns that prevail in the following areas: TV advertising, industrial relations, newspapers, holiday travel, house purchase and wearing jeans.

Lateral thinking

There are two types of progress. One is fast, the other is very slow.

The first type of progress is illustrated below. We are going along and a technical input or an idea allows us to move faster. Another input accelerates our progress even further – and so on. There are people alive today who were born before the first aeroplane flew. Some time ago, on a journey across the Atlantic, I reflected that the spoonful of mashed potato I was about to put into my mouth was actually travelling faster than a rifle bullet. So were the other passengers on the Concorde. Extraordinary progress in a very short time.

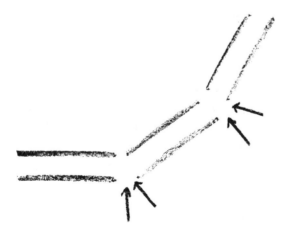

Today at a cost of about $5,000 we can have on our desks a computer that is more powerful than the first computer which cost about $5 million (in today's terms) and filled three rooms.

In fact we can have a pretty powerful personal computer for as little as $130. That also is amazing progress.

Then there is the other type of progress. Our experience forms certain concepts, patterns and organisations. We follow along this pattern. In order to progress we may have to back track and change to another pattern which is more appropriate for the conditions. But we have no mechanisms for this backtracking or changing patterns. So progress is excruciatingly slow. This is the sort of progress that we get in the social area as contrasted with the technical area. It is no one's fault. That is the way our minds work. That is the way organisations work. They are summaries of the past, not designs for the future. This slower type of progress is illustrated here.

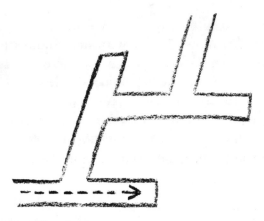

Pattern changing

In the previous section we looked at the marvellous system the brain has for creating and using patterns. This allows us to make sense of the world and to live. Without such a system, life would be impossible. The main purpose of the brain is to be brilliantly uncreative. And so it should be. But from time to time a change of pattern is required. This is difficult because we do not really have any mechanisms for doing this. In the political sense we have the extraordinarily wasteful and inefficient 'clash' system. In science and thought we have tended also to use this method — for lack of anything better.

In medicine most of the major discoveries have come about through chance observation, accident or mistake. This is hardly surprising because, in a system as complex as the body, systematic search is not possible. Once the 'break' has occurred then the scientific method can follow through with its analysis and development.

In terms of the mind, the mechanisms for pattern changing are mistake, accident and humour. It is difficult to see what other mechanisms there could be. Working within existing patterns will not itself lead to new patterns.

Humour

It has always amazed me how little attention philosophers, psychologists and information theorists have paid to humour. Humour is probably the most significant characteristic of the human mind. It tells us much more about how the system works than does anything else. Reason tells us very little and we can devise reasoning systems with pebbles, beads on an abacus, cogwheels or electronics. But humour can only occur in a self-organising patterning system of the sort we find in human perception.

Humour involves the escape from one pattern and the switching into another.

Below, I have drawn a major track or pattern and a side track. It is a characteristic of patterning systems that as we move along the main track the side track is, for the moment, inaccessible (for an explanation of this see my book *The Mechanism of Mind*). So we go shooting past along the main track.

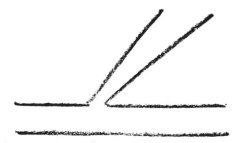

In the pun type of humour the double meaning of a word is used as the pattern-switching device to force us along the side track.

Consider the following puns:
'Bob Hope had a bad Christmas. He was only given three golf clubs. What is worse only two of them had swimming pools.'
'Two healthy young ladies went for a tramp in the woods, but the tramp got away.'

The other mechanism of humour is shown in the next drawing. In this mechanism we are taken to an apparently unreasonable point and suddenly see our way back. For example:
'The ticket inspector came into the train compartment. The young man began to search frantically for his ticket: top pockets, trouser pockets, back pocket, coat on the rack, briefcase and everywhere. After a while the inspector took pity on him and extracted the ticket from the young man's mouth where it had been all along. When the inspector had left, another passenger asked the young man if he felt foolish. "Not at all," said the young man, "I was chewing the date off the ticket".'

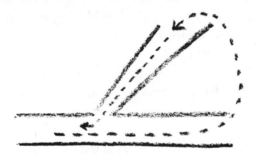

Hindsight and insight

The pattern switching that we observe in humour is exactly the same process that occurs in hindsight and insight. We switch to a new pattern and suddenly see that something is reasonable and obvious. In hindsight any creative idea must be logical – otherwise we could never accept it as having value. The mistake we make is to assume that since it is logical in hindsight then the better exercise of logic could have got us there in the first place. This mistake is only made by people who do not understand the nature of patterning systems. Patterning systems are necessarily asymmetric – otherwise they would be quite useless. In the figure below the route from A to B is very different from the route from B to A.

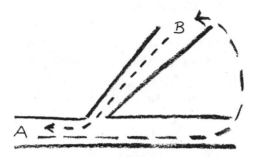

The purpose of lateral thinking is to provide a more deliberate means for pattern-switching than relying on mistake or accident. Lateral thinking seeks to achieve the pattern-switching that occurs in insight.

Creativity and lateral thinking

I am often asked why it was necessary to invent the term 'lateral thinking' when the word 'creativity' seemed quite adequate. The answer is that the word 'creativity' is far from adequate and does not describe what I mean by lateral thinking. That may be why the term 'lateral thinking' is now included in the *Oxford English Dictionary*.

A creative person may have a way of looking at the world which is different from the way other people see the world, as illustrated below.

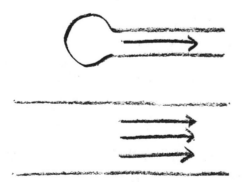

If that person is successful in expressing and communicating his own special perception, then we call him or her creative and value the contribution that takes some of us to see the world through a new perspective. We acknowledge the creativity. But that person may be locked into that special perception: unable to change perception or see the world in any other way. Thus many creative people are actually 'rigid' at the same time. This does not at all diminish their value to society and their ability to create within their special perception. But in 'lateral thinking' I am interested in the ability to change perception and to keep on changing perception. Clearly such people are indeed creative but not lateral thinkers. Some creative people are both.

The same thing happens with young children. If a youngster of about nine is given a problem, he may well come up with a highly original solution since he is not trapped within the conventional approach. So his approach is creative and original. But that same youngster may be reluctant to look for, and unable to find, a different approach. So he is creative and original and also rigid.

Lateral thinking can be precisely defined as pattern-switching within a patterning system. To explain the nature of a patterning system takes quite a long time. So in ordinary terms we can describe it as the ability to look at things in different ways.

Grandma is knitting and young Susie is disturbing Grandma by playing with the ball of wool. The father suggests putting Susie in the play-pen. The mother suggests that it might make more sense to put Grandma in the play-pen – a different way of looking at things which is quite logical in hindsight.

Lateral thinking as process

Another difficulty with the word 'creativity' is that it is a value judgement. No one has ever called a new idea which he or she personally did not like, 'creative'. Lateral thinking is a neutral process.

Sometimes we use it and come up with nothing at all. Some times we use it and come up with a good idea but one that is no better than the existing idea. Sometimes (occasionally) we use it and come up with a new idea that is much better than the existing one. In all three cases we are using lateral thinking.

Intelligent people often tend to be conformists. They learn the rules of the game and make use of them to have a comfortable life. At school they learn the rules of the game: how to please teacher; how to pass exams with minimal work; how to get on with people. Creativity tends to be left to the rebels who cannot or will not play the rules for a variety of reasons. The paradox is that if we treat creativity (in the form of lateral thinking) as a perfectly sober part of information processing then we may get the strange effect of the conformists being more creative than the rebels – because the conformists are also better at playing the rules of creativity. If creativity is no longer a risk then non-risk takers may decide to be creative.

Lateral thinking is both an attitude of mind and also a number of defined methods. The attitude of mind involves the willingness to try to look at things in different ways. It involves an appreciation that any way of looking at things is only one amongst many possible ways. It involves an understanding of how the mind uses patterns and the need to escape from an established pattern in order to switch into a better one. There is no mystique about it.

Judgement and provocation

In my seminars I often use a drawing of the strange wheelbarrow shown below. I ask the audience to write down, individually, five comments on the design. Invariably the comments criticise the design: the wheel is in the wrong place; the wheel-bearing strut would break off; the wheel is too small; the barrow would tip over; the handles are too short; it is more difficult to press down than to lift – and so on.

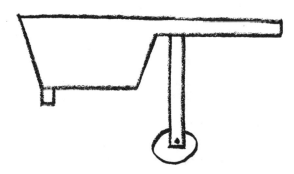

The ratio of negative comments to 'interested' comments has been: for executives, 20 to 1; for a group all of whom had an IQ of over 140, 22 to 1; for a group of teachers, 27 to 1; for a group of 12 to 13 year olds, 2 to 1. The low figure shown for the youngsters reflected two things: first, they did not know much about wheelbarrows, centres of gravity, leverage or those sorts of things; second, they thought it was the best wheelbarrow I could manage and they were motivated to be nice to me. The 'interested' comments were many and varied: good barrow for filling holes and ditches because you could come to the edge and release the floor of the bin so avoiding the need to tip; better for turning sharp corners as on scaffolding, because the turning circle is smaller; you could not strain your back because if you tried to lift more than your own weight you would take off; you could have the wheel-bearing strut moving telescopically against a spring and, by painting the upper part of the strut red and the bottom part green, you could now tell how hard a person was working depending on the colour you saw as he went by.

The adults were, correctly, using judgement. In order to operate a patterning system we do have to use judgement.

We use judgement for recognition and identification (as we saw in the last section). We use judgement to find out which pattern we are using. Then we also use judgement to stop us wandering off the pattern. So all the negative comments of the adults were based on their proper use of judgement. That is why the teachers got a somewhat higher score than the others.

I believe that people ought to use judgement. Without it we could not get by. A patterning system cannot work without the use of judgement.

But we also need to create another idiom. This is the idiom of 'movement'. Movement is for moving across channels (as suggested in the figure opposite). So we use judgement for staying within existing channels but are also able to use 'movement' when we want to change patterns. It is no different from having different gears in your car. You use one gear for starting, another for cruising, a third for reversing, So, in our thinking we ought to be able to use judgement when we want to and movement when we want to. That is what the 'skill' of thinking is all about.

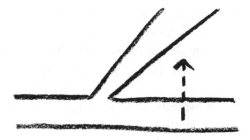

The figure below illustrates what we mean by 'movement'.

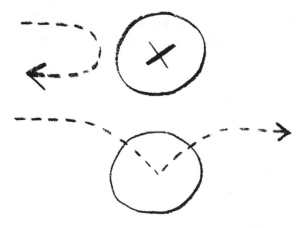

In the judgement idiom, when we come to an idea which is wrong we condemn it and back away. In the movement idiom we use the idea for its 'movement value'. This means using it as a stepping stone to help us move to a different pattern. It means using it to see where it will lead to, what it might suggest. It is *not* that we treat a bad idea as a good idea. It is that we are operating outside the judgement system, and irrespective of whether the idea is good or bad we want to use it for its movement value. Movement value is 'provocation'.

The word 'po'

I invented the word 'po' many years ago. It is derived from such words as: hypothesis, suppose, possible and poetry. The syllable 'po' is in all these. Also all these words describe the 'forward use' of an idea: what does the idea lead on to? In all these cases the idea is put forward to see what effect it will have on our thinking. In a sense they are all provocative rather than descriptive situations. The word 'po' is directly and deliberately provocative and therefore stronger than all of them. For example, an hypothesis should be somewhat reasonable, but a po provocation can be consciously illogical. For simplicity 'po' can be read as standing for '*p*rovocative *o*peration'.

Why do we need po? Simply as an indication to ourselves and to others that, for the moment, we are operating in the 'movement' system and not in the 'judgement' system. There is no magic about it. Like any notation it is designed for convenience.

Po is not the same as 'maybe' or the Japanese 'mu'. It is not a matter of suspending judgement or being unwilling to judge. It is a matter of operating *outside* the judgement system.

The best definition of provocation is as follows:
"There may not be a reason for saying something until after it has been said".

The stepping stone method

The figure below shows how we use the movement value of a stepping stone in order to make easier our switch from one pattern to another.

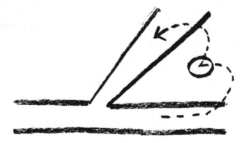

On one occasion we were considering the problem of traffic parking in a small town where commuters tended to park in the centre and so block the spaces that would otherwise be used by shoppers. Parking meters could have solved the problem. We wanted a simpler solution.

The provocation was: 'Po cars would limit their own parking'. From this came the notion that anyone could park anywhere for as long as he or she liked – provided the headlights were left on. So parking would be self-limiting. In a way this idea could be applied in towns with meters. If you left your headlights on you would be indicating that you were only there for a few minutes and so would not need to pay the meter fee. This would give a greater turn-over of meter spaces.

On another occasion the problem was river pollution by factories sited along the river. The further down river you were, the greater the pollution of the water reaching you. The provocation on this occasion was: 'the Po factory should be downstream of itself.' This is an illogical statement at first sight. Yet its 'movement value' led quite quickly to an idea which has been implemented (so I am told) in some countries. Normally the factory's input is upstream of its output. The provocation leads directly to the suggestion that legislation should insist that the factory's input would be downstream of its own output – so that it would be the first to suffer from failure to clean up the effluent.

In a seminar I once put forward the absurd provocation: 'Po aeroplanes should land upside down.' This is an example of the simplest form of deliberate provocation: the reversal. You take the way something is normally done and then reverse it to create the provocation. Other methods of obtaining provocations include exaggeration, distortion, wishful thinking (as in the examples of car parking and river pollution) and the outrageous. Those seeking more detailed information on the techniques of lateral thinking should see the book *Lateral Thinking: a textbook of creativity*. The provocation that planes should land upside down led to the consideration that the pilot would have a much better view. This in turn led to consideration of where the pilot should be placed. Was being on top the best place or only the traditional one (from the days when planes were much smaller)?

The provocation, 'Po cars should have square wheels' has led to about twelve different lines of thought about cars and wheels, including the following:

- o an inner tyre at normal pressure and an outer one at low pressure so giving better adhesion
- o a bolt on 'square' wheel to be fixed on to the normal wheel in conditions of snow, mud or sand
- o a vehicle which flowed over bumps instead of bumping over them by means of an adjustable suspension and a forward jockey wheel
- o a spiral tread for tyres so avoiding aquaplaning problems
- o special 'braking wheels' for heavy vehicles which would normally be out of contact with the road but which would be forced down hydraulically in emergencies
- o separate design for driving wheels and trailing wheels
- o cars that would ratchet up into a semi-vertical position for better use of parking space
- o segmented tyres to reduce blow-out and puncture problems
- o variable geometry or variable inflation tyres
  . . . and so on.

The reader is invited to carry the same provocation further.

Provocations can be obtained in this deliberate manner or else they may arise in the course of thinking or conversation. An idea which is at first rejected may be used, for a while, as a provocation. In other words the movement idiom is used as well as the judgement idiom.

Movement is obtained in a variety of ways: by extracting the principle of the idea; by following the moment-to-moment consequences; by focusing on the difference from the usual; by spelling out the positive aspects.

The escape method

Here the effort is to identify the main track of our thinking and then to escape from this main track.

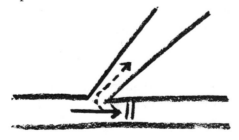

In practice it is extremely difficult to identify those things we take for granted in a situation. To obtain the escape we try dropping a particular feature or altering it or finding an alternative way of achieving the same end.

The phrase 'take for granted' is one of the ways of identifying our normal patterns. For example, if we were looking at telephone booths or kiosks we 'take for granted' that they are all the same price. An escape might lead us to the notion of having one high-priced telephone amongst a row of others. This would tend to be empty so that a person with an urgent call to make would be more likely to find a telephone – and would not mind paying the higher price. We also take for granted that there is one telephone in each booth. Suppose we put two telephones there. What would be of interest or benefit in this idea? If one phone was out of order the other one could be used. You could make calls whilst waiting for someone to ring you back. At very busy times and if the cord were long enough, two people could use the phones.

In London, there are relatively few taxis (about 11,000 compared to 15,000 in Moscow and 30,000 in New York). To obtain a taxi-driving licence a driver has to pass the 'knowledge' exam which involves detailed knowledge of streets, embassies, hotels etc. It takes several months to acquire this knowledge and no one pays the learner. What do we take for granted about taxi-drivers? That they know the way. As an alteration we 'po' a taxi driver who does not know the way. What would he do? He might ask someone. Whom might he ask? His passenger. At this point we are in sight of an interesting idea.

There would be the usual taxis, exactly as at present. They would be used by tourists and out-of-towners. Then there would be another type of taxi distinguished by the large question mark on the roof – indicating that the driver did not know his way about. By definition this type would be restricted to residents who did know the way about and could instruct the driver. The driver could thus be earning money even as he learned his way about (if he had to find his way back without a fare he would use a map or a telephone). So there would be more taxis both immediately and eventually. Residents and visitors would both benefit. Learner taxi-drivers would benefit.

We take for granted that there should be but one currency in each country. There are some interesting economic possibilities of escaping from this concept: for example to have two currencies one of which is indexed against the other so providing a sort of internal gold-standard.

As an exercise try to identify some pattern we take for granted in the following situations. Make an attempt to escape from that pattern and then follow along to see what benefit or interest arises from your escape. The situations are: a car steering wheel, voting in an election, book publishing, cheques, a frying pan and traffic lights.

There are many other ways of using the 'escape method'. As before, those who want more details should consult the book *Lateral Thinking: a textbook of creativity*.

The random stimulation method

This is the easiest method of all. It is also the most fun. It is now used in a formal manner by most of the major advertising agencies in the world. The random stimulation is provided by a random object or word or person or magazine or exhibition. The main thing is that it cannot be chosen because if it is chosen then it is chosen through its relevance to current ideas and therefore will reinforce rather than change them. It is a matter of exposing oneself to a random influence or deliberately producing one.

The most convenient form is a random word. You can get a random word by specifying a page number in a dictionary and then the position of the word on that page. You count down until you come to the word. To make it easier you can continue until you come to the nearest noun.

For example, I was once discussing the training of teachers for a country that rapidly needed a lot more teachers. The dictionary page number and the position of the word on the page gave 'tadpole' which has no obvious relevance to teacher training. The visual concept that comes from a tadpole is that of the tail. So we might say 'Po teachers have tails.' In practice what might that mean? It could mean having two assistants or apprentices who followed the teacher around and eventually came to take over more and more functions. In this way each teacher could be multiplied twice over. Training colleges could still be set up and teachers brought in for in-service training later on.

The random word serves to tap into lines of thought that might otherwise have been hidden. The association of traffic lights with cigarettes produced the notion of a red band around the cigarette, 1.5 centimetres from the butt end, to indicate that the smoker was entering the most dangerous zone and to give him the option of discarding that cigarette.

At first sight it seems illogical to suppose that a random word will help in any problem (which must follow if the word is truly random). In a patterning system, however, it makes sense. If you lived in London and I dropped you in any part of London you would eventually find your way home (your knowledge, maps, asking directions). As you arrived home you might find yourself approaching it from a direction quite different from the one you normally used on leaving home. That is exactly how the random word works. This is illustrated below. In our thinking we move out of a certain area along the traditional route. If we toss in a random word it has its own associations. Sooner or later these link up with the associations of the 'problem'. We can now move out of the 'problem' along this new route and see what we find.

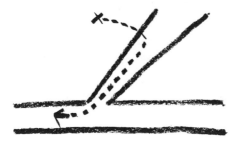

In practice it does sometimes happen that the association of the random word is so close that little provocation is obtained. It has never happened that the word is too remote. This is not so surprising because we follow the associations of the word and this opens up other words until a large fan of 'connectors' is obtained. We may also extract a function from the word. For example, the word 'elephant' might give the function 'very large', and clearly this can be applied to most situations.

Several people have told me how by using the random word they have designed important new products in a variety of fields: financial services, household products, bridge construction etc. As an exercise try to use the following random words to produce some new ideas in the given area.

o random word 'frog' – area is medical care
o random word 'tennis racket' – area is kitchen design
o random word 'policy' – area is hair shampoo
o random word 'vote' – area is traffic control
o random word 'volcano' – area is camera design
o random word 'soap' – area is house purchase financing.

General use of lateral thinking

The three methods: 'stepping stone', 'escape' and 'random stimulation' can be used as specific and formal methods for generating a new idea or a new approach. What is even more important is the lateral thinking attitude which involves the willingness to search for better concepts. In a sense each of the methods illustrates an aspect of the lateral thinking attitude. In the 'stepping-stone' method we treat an idea for its movement value instead of just its judgement value. This is a positive, constructive attitude. In the 'escape' method we focus on things we take for granted and wonder whether they are indeed the only or best way of doing things. We are willing to improve them or escape from them. In the 'random stimulation' method we open ourselves to influences other than those we directly look for. We allow ourselves to be stimulated.

The logic of lateral thinking

If we consider the behaviour of self-organising patterning systems in perception then the logic of lateral thinking follows. Lateral thinking is quite logical in the universe of patterning systems. We need methods for cutting across patterns instead of just moving up and down them.

Lateral thinking is to do with change, especially when change involves escaping from a pattern that has been satisfactory in the past. In another section in this book I shall be looking at our more normal method of change, which is through criticism and attack. The weakness of that method is that we can only consider change when a concept can be shown to be inadequate and when the attacking party has the power to carry through the change.

The Japanese have never had the 'clash' or dialectic system which we value so highly in the West. They are therefore much more interested in change through exploration, insight and switching. This is very much the idiom of lateral thinking. That may be why all my books are translated into Japanese and why the *per capita* sales are far higher than anywhere else in the world. It should also be noted that the security of their existing patterns, far from preventing idea changes, actually gives them the freedom to explore. They seem to use tradition as a base for change rather than as a bulwark against change.

Information
and
thinking

There is one being who cannot think – and cannot have a sense of humour.

That being is, of course, God. Thinking involves moving from one state of knowledge to a better one. Since God has perfect knowledge he is always there already. So thinking is not only superfluous but impossible. Nor can God have a sense of humour since there can be no surprise when the punch-lines have always been known.

It is only our lack of complete information that makes it necessary for us to think.

In education we try to approach the God-like state of complete information. That gets harder and harder as there is more and more information to absorb. The idiom is that of information supply. Thinking is no substitute for information. Check the time-table, do not just try to think when there might be a flight to Geneva.

The more information we have the better will our thinking be and the more appropriate our actions. Since every little bit of information helps, every bit of time must be taken up with providing more information. So there is no time to look directly at thinking as a skill.

The dilemma is obvious. If we could have complete information in an area then thinking is unnecessary. But if we cannot have complete information then it is rather better to have somewhat less information and a higher skill in thinking. This dilemma is illustrated below. Simply stated the dilemma is this: if we cannot have complete information should we spend time on more information or on thinking skills?

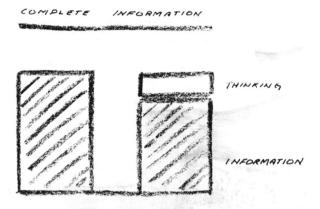

There may be certain areas where it is possible to have complete information but more often we have to supplement the information with thinking. Suppose the time-table does show that there is a flight from London to Geneva at 9.45 a.m. designated as SR 815. Now that we know, do we need thinking? Indeed, we do. How are we going to get to the airport? How long should we allow to get there? Is it peak traffic time? Are there any strikes on at the moment? Is there likely to be bad weather and what would be the best way of checking this? Does it matter if the flight is late? If the plans are disrupted how do I let the person at the other end know of this? These are all considerations that require thinking.

Operacy

There is one area where we can never have complete information and where we must use our thinking. That area is the 'future'. All our actions, plans, decisions and choices are going to be worked out in the future. In short, the future is where 'action' takes place. Education, however, is essentially about the past. It is a matter of sorting, reviewing, describing and absorbing existing knowledge. The supposition is that if we can get together enough information then action is obvious and easy. But the skills of doing require much more. They require thinking about priorities, about the consequences of action and about the other people involved. These are all aspects of the CoRT thinking lessons. I have coined the term 'operacy' for the skills of doing. I believe that in schools it should rank equally with numeracy and literacy.

Quite a lot of the thinking involved in 'doing' requires the application of experience to the current situation.

Experience scan

If all our experience were to be instantly available we should be much better thinkers. But it is not, and we have to direct our attention carefully over our experience in order to pick out what we need for the moment. One of the major faults of thinking is what we call 'point-to-point' thinking in which the mind drifts from point to point without any systematic scan. Twenty-four groups of youngsters in the London area were asked to consider the suggestion that 'bread, fish and milk should be free'. The youngsters were aged 11. Twenty-three of the groups decided that it was a bad suggestion even though some of them came from families so poor that they could only afford milk occasionally. A typical example of the point-to-point thinking went as follows: 'If they were free everyone would want them. The shops would be crowded. The buses would be crowded. The drivers would want more money. They would not get more money. They would go on strike. Other people would go on strike. So it's a bad idea.' Each point has a connection with the next point but there is no scan around the suggestion itself.

Since our experience, including the information we have learned, is the major source of information that we bring to bear on a matter, we need to develop general purpose scanning tools. Two such tools are 'CAF' (Consider All Factors) and 'C & S' (Consequence and Sequel). These tools were designed to counter the tendency for thinking to be ego-centric and very short-term.

CAF

This is an attention-directing tool like the PMI and APC. In other words, a device to make concrete what would otherwise remain a general intention to look broadly around an issue. 'Doing a CAF' means considering all the factors that have to be considered in a situation. There is no attempt to evaluate the factors. For example doing a CAF on buying a secondhand car might result in the following items: price, previous history, previous owners, present owner, mileage, likelihood of mileage having been altered, re-sale value, comparison of price with official listings and other vendors, state of the car, petrol consumption, oil consumption, state of the tyres, rust, state of the road worthiness certificate, suitability of the car, cost of spares, nearness of service agent, and so on. This is not a complete list, nor are the items in order of priority. Some of them even overlap. For example, the 'state of the car' could include such items as 'rust' and 'state of the tyres'. If anything is to get individual attention it is worth listing separately. Whilst general headings include many factors they do not serve to direct attention to each of these factors – so a separate listing is helpful.

In doing a CAF the emphasis is on 'what has been left out?' and 'what ought we to consider as well?'. A young couple who buy a large bed and find that it will not go through the front door have left out a major consideration.

Do a CAF on the following: choosing a place to live; buying a carpet; painting a room; buying a book as a present; choosing a newspaper; designing a TV programme; choosing an item on the menu.

C & S

Thinking is almost always short-term because the attraction or repulsion of a course of action is immediate. We are interested in what happens next: the future can look after itself. As we shall see in the later section on values and emotions, society has created all sorts of devices to make us think in a more long-term fashion.

The C & S thinking task is an instruction deliberately to consider the consequences of an action or decision. Four time zones are suggested: immediate consequences up to 1 year; short-term from 1 to 5 years; medium-term from 5 to 20 years; long-term over 20 years. These time frames are arbitrary and can be varied. They can also be specified to suit the situation.

In doing a C & S there is the usual deliberate attempt to focus on the frame of the moment. Just as in the PMI the thinker focuses on the Plus, Minus and Interesting aspects in turn, so in the C & S the different time zones are focused upon in turn. The exercise is surprisingly difficult, partly because it is unnatural. The difficulty also arises from our reluctance to assign time zones. We can appreciate that a consequence may happen 'sometime' but be very hazy as to when that might be. The C & S is a usable tool for getting rid of that haziness.

For example a C & S on a major break-through in solar energy technology could show the following.

Immediate (up to 1 year): rapid change in stock market prices of companies involved; a great deal of talk and speculation; slight fall in oil prices; new designs for buildings show provision for solar energy panels.

Short-term (1 to 5 years): further fall in oil prices; much less development than expected; property prices in desert cities start to rise; Third World countries borrow money for big schemes.

Medium-term (5 to 20 years): some projects are operating, others have failed; better appreciation of those areas where solar energy is most useful; two further steps in the technology; oil prices are now beginning to rise again; hydrogen is being tried as fuel for cars.

Long-term (over 20 years): sharp division of energy uses according to pricing and convenience; solar energy beginning to have major use except with transportation systems; price of oil rising faster – for transportation and chemical feed-stocks.

As an exercise, do a C & S on the following suggestions: office work can be done at home via computer terminals; air travel becomes too expensive for holidays; the invention of a harmless happiness pill.

The experience scan that is attempted with such tools as CAF and C & S is part of the general broadening of perception that has more to do with wisdom than with cleverness. It should be noted that with the C & S there can be no certainty on any of the points: all thinking about the future is speculative and is based on 'may be' and 'could be' even though these may have different degrees of likeliness.

Dense reading and dense listening

Very few people are good listeners. A good listener listens slowly to what is being said. He does not jump ahead nor does he rush to judge nor does he sit there formulating his own reply. He focuses directly on what is being said. He listens to more than is being said. He extracts the maximum information from what he hears by looking between the words used and wondering why something has been expressed in a particular way. It is active listening because the listener's imagination is full of 'could be' and 'may be' elaborations.

Dense reading is like dense listening. The reader reads between the lines and considers all the implications of what has been read. It is the opposite of fast reading, which is only interested in the broad thrust of what is being offered. If you want to find out what happens and want to get to the end of the story quickly then you are not using dense reading. Both styles of reading have their place and their value. As usual the skill of thinking lies in knowing which skill to use at any particular time.

Dense reading involves a lot of thinking. Implications can often only be seen if our thinking creates a number of possible situations around what is being read.

Consider the implications of the following remark which I once made to a class in Barcelona: 'It seems to me that there are a lot of shoe shops in Barcelona.' The implications could include the following.

o that I had visited that part of town where the shoe shops were located
o that I had probably walked rather than gone by car
o that there was a part of town with a large number of shoe shops
o that I may have wanted to buy some shoes or had other special interest in shoe shops
o that there were good profit margins on shoes in Spain

- o that people wore more shoes
- o that tourists bought shoes in Barcelona
- o that shoes wore out more quickly
- o that there were no very big shoe shops or stores
- o that business property taxes were low in Barcelona
- o that there were few shoe shops in other parts of town.

Most of these are highly speculative and on the basis of 'it could be that . . .'. With a single statement that is as far as things could go. When there is a whole passage to be read then the overlap of these expanded speculations can start to form into something more definite. For example, if the passage went on to mention high property prices in Barcelona then it would seem likely either that people bought a lot of shoes or that the profit margins were high. Similarly if Barcelona was mentioned as a tourist centre then this would increase the likelihood of larger sales of shoes.

There is no special trick about dense reading and dense listening except to *want* to do it.

Logic

Logic is a way of generating information. It is a way of extracting more information from what is available. For example, we may not know if there is a road from A to C. But we do know that there is a road from A to B. We also know that there is a road from B to C. By putting these two pieces of information together we can infer that it must be possible to get from A to C.

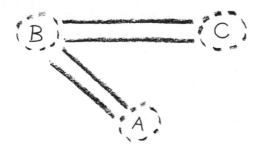

The classification type logic mentioned earlier in the book is another aid to getting more information. Once we can show that something is a member of a group we can then infer that the thing has all the properties of the group. As mentioned before, this is a somewhat circular matter (because we should not really have put the thing into the group unless we already knew it had all the properties of the group) but it does have a practical utility – especially when dealing with words rather than the things of the world.

Another aspect of logic is to construct a particular type of information universe (as in mathematics) and then to explore the relationships that occur in this universe. The danger lies in transferring conclusions from these special universes to the real world.

For example, in a spherical universe we may simultaneously be moving away from A and towards A at the same time (or on a circular railway track). This apparently contradicts the law of contradiction.

In the speculative areas discussed in this section the operative words were 'could be' and 'may be'. Logic seeks to be much more certain than that and here the terms are 'must be' and 'cannot be'. Instead of overlapping fields of possibility we seek to move from one step to another with the certainty of deduction.

Where the system works it can be most effective, but it is not as easily applicable to the real world as many would claim.

Getting more information

So far we have considered getting better use out of the information we already possess. Getting more information from outside can involve three things: use of information sources; questions; experiments.

The use of information sources is a whole area in itself – and often one which is not given sufficient attention. Knowing where to look and how to look is just as important as any thinking skill. It should be treated somewhat like problem solving: knowing where you want to end up and exploring the ways of getting there.

Questions

The skilled use of questions is the lawyer's main tool. Broadly speaking, questions fall into two types. First, there is the 'shooting question' (SQ) in which we know exactly what we are aiming at. We usually expect a 'yes' or a 'no' for an answer, or at least the question could have been phrased to obtain such an answer. We may wish to have something confirmed or denied. For example: 'Did you go to London yesterday?' The term 'shooting' is used because we know what we are aiming at.

With a 'fishing question' (FQ) we dangle the bait in the water and wait to see what we catch. 'Where did you go, yesterday?' is a fishing question because we do not know what the answer might be. Fishing questions are used to open up a situation. They are also used when the number of imagined possibilities is so large that it would take a whole series of shooting questions to narrow them down. Even within fishing questions there is a degree of focus. For example the question 'What did you do yesterday?' is more open than 'Where did you go yesterday?'

It is obviously impossible to ask a question without some intention behind it. The important thing is to define that intention and then to work out a way of furthering it. Devising questions is not as easy as it sometimes seems. It is easy enough to ask any old question, but to ask questions efficiently and economically is another matter. There is an elegance to it.

As an exercise construct a short series (in each case) of shooting and fishing questions to elicit the information required in each of the following situations. The questioning must be tactful.

o You want to know why a man, who has come to you for a job, has left his last job.
o You want to know if the doctor who has just seen you has any idea of the diagnosis.
o You want to know from an estate agent whether the price you are thinking of offering for a house is too high or too low.
o You want to know whether your daughter's teacher thinks she is bright or not.

Experiments

An experiment is a question that we ask of the environment. It is usually a shooting question in the sense that the experiment will work or it will not. We do have certain hopes and expectations. There is a simple game which can tell us a lot about how to devise experiments. A person makes a simple drawing which contains a 'hidden' feature. The experimenter has to find out what the feature is by doing 'experiments'. An experiment consists of another drawing. If the other drawing also contains the 'hidden' feature then the experiment 'works' and is ticked as correct. If it does not contain the feature it fails and is marked with a cross.

An interesting example of this game is shown here.

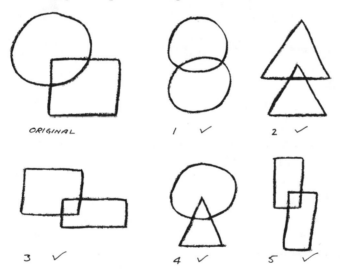

ORIGINAL   1 ✓   2 ✓

3 ✓   4 ✓   5 ✓

The original drawing is shown and then a whole series of experiments, all of which are correct. The experimenter, however, has not got much further. Contrast this series with this drawing.

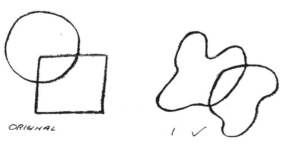

ORIGINAL   1 ✓

With just one experiment the experimenter has got further than the first experimenter. The shapeless shape that is marked as correct immediately excludes the necessity for any regular shape. This is a 'big jump' experiment. The hypothesis is a bold one. It immediately excludes a whole range of possibilities which would otherwise have had to be tested one by one.

As with the design of questions the design of experiments needs careful thought. What is the most that can be got from an experiment: the most certainty, the most information?

Negative information is important. In some cases negative information is even more important than positive information because negative information can exclude a whole range of possibilities.

Selecting information

The problems set so neatly in mathematical textbooks provide all the information that is needed. The student is encouraged to use all the information supplied. Life, however, is never as neat as that. Sometimes there is not enough information to solve the problem. Sometimes there may even be too much. In one of my books, *The Five Day Course in Thinking*, I set a problem involving the construction of a bridge of knives that had to support a glass of water between some bottles. I said that four knives could be used. In fact the problem could be solved with just three knives. I received a lot of furious letters telling me that I had cheated by saying that four knives could be used when three would do.

Selecting out the relevant information is an important part of information thinking. This becomes even more important when obtaining the information is going to cost time, money and effort.

FI–FO

This is another of the CoRT thinking tools, and it stands for inFormation-In and inFormation-Out. It is a deliberate survey of what is already available and that which is still required.

The information already available is examined carefully in the 'dense' manner suggested earlier in this section. All the implications and logical inferences are extracted from it. This is the 'FI' part.

Then the 'gaps' in the formation are examined. It is not easy to see gaps because they have to be inferred. We have to imagine what information is required in order to see that it is not available. These gaps are defined and spelled out carefully. There should be as much consciousness of the information that is not available as there is of the information that is available.

For exercise do a FI–FO on the following situations. In this case list the information which would usually be available and that which would usually be left out.

o Choosing a new place to go for a holiday
o Borrowing money to buy a house
o Buying a board game
o Giving a party.

Two uses

We need both information and thinking. Information is no substitute for thinking and thinking is no substitute for information.
In connection with information there are two uses for our thinking. The first is directed at the information itself: getting information; obtaining the maximum from the information we already have; checking the information. The second is the use of the information to carry out some thinking purpose: decision, action, choice, planning, design or pleasure.

Other people

Most thinking is not to do with puzzles and games. Most thinking is to do with other people.

It is therefore unfortunate that Western civilisation has developed – and continues very much to encourage – a type of thinking that is wasteful, inefficient and getting ever more dangerous. Western civilisation in its philosophy and in its practice has been obsessed with the 'clash' system in which two opposing views fight it out. This covers argument, debate, the adversary system in general and dialectics. The method pervades our politics, our courts, our business decisions and day to day living. We really do believe that from a clash of opposing views a better one will emerge. We have even adopted this as our only method of change.

The disadvantages of the clash system are many. As one side attacks and the other side defends, each point of view grows ever more rigid and unable to develop. This is suggested in the figure below. The need to attack and defend precludes more useful thinking. This may be why I have found politicians, as a group, less interested in thinking and new ideas than any other group (not excluding Church groups).

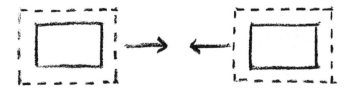

In the clash system one or other point of view will eventually prevail, as in a political election. The other group is bitter and disappointed and unwilling to make the new system work. Since in a large number of elections the losers are actually more than the winners this bitterness matters a great deal. This disappointment is suggested in the figure below.

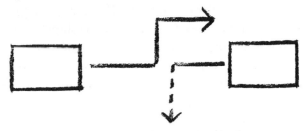

In most areas the major defect of the clash system is that in order to even begin to think about change, the existing idea must first be attacked. Not only must it be attacked, but it must be shown to be inadequate. This is the most complete nonsense imaginable. An idea may have been a good one in its time and may still be a good idea. But this does not preclude the possibility of a much better idea. We may never be able to prove the existing idea inadequate (especially when working from within the concepts created by that idea) so we are never able to explore for change. Another huge disadvantage of this method is that if we have to destroy the existing idea in order to start looking for a better idea, then, if we do not find a better idea, we have nothing to come back to. We are left without a base. This is one of the great dangers of adversary politics in which each side spends so much time attacking the other that the credibility of both is destroyed. There are no winners in that sort of argument. In the Japanese system, as mentioned earlier, the security of the present patterns do not have to be attacked before there can be any exploration for change. This not only saves time and channels mental effort into better directions but it also means that until a better idea is found the existing base is still valued.

It is not too difficult to see how this strange habit of Western thought emerged. In medieval times thinking and learning were in the hands of the church – as was civilisation. Everyone else was too busy killing or being killed. The church ran the schools and universities and provided the thinkers. Quite *correctly*, the main function of the thinkers of the church was to preserve the existing theology because in those days theology was taken very seriously. Preserving this theology meant attacking and annihilating the many heresies which were forever springing up. This was a hard task because many of the heretics were very bright people too. So there developed an emphasis on the skills of argument and destructive criticism. All this was perfectly in order and a valid use of thinking. If you could prove the heresy to be nonsense you preserved intact your theology. Since theology is expressed in words the arguments were semantic arguments and a type of thinking emerged which is actually only applicable to semantic argument (scholastic philosophy). All this was very much helped by the discovery of Greek philosophy and such things as the Socratic dialogue.

So the clash system emerged. Since the Church controlled schools and universities this idiom became the idiom of Western thinking. Because universities and schools appoint successors in their own image, the idiom has continued to this day, to the extent that in an editorial in recent years *The Times* declared what so many believe, that the exercise of the critical intelligence was the aim of education, Forgetting that for criticism to have any value there must be a great deal of constructive thinking going on somewhere.

It is easy to see why the clash system is so appealing. Negative criticism offers the opportunity for a great deal of apparent thinking. It is the refuge both of the mediocre mind and also – alas – of the brilliant mind. The mediocre mind that is incapable of doing anything else finds criticism easy since it is one of the cheapest forms of thinking. By that I mean that you can criticise anything at all by just choosing a frame different from what you see. For example, if the designer has produced a simple chair you call it 'stark', 'boring', 'prison-like'. Now if the designer had produced a more elaborate chair you would just have shifted your frame of expectation and called it 'fussy', 'pretentious' and 'over-elaborate' (even 'vulgar').

When I first suggested in the columns of the *Times Educational Supplement* many years ago that thinking should be taught directly as a skill in schools there was a wave of protest saying that it should not be done and could not be done. When I reported a year later that it was actually being done there was very little interest. Not so long ago a certain professor sat down and decided that the CoRT material could not possibly work – ignoring the fact that it was working in thousands of schools and had been for years, including schools quite near to him.

So negative criticism offers an easy form of activity to mediocre minds. Unfortunately it also offers an attraction to brilliant minds, as mentioned earlier in the 'intelligence trap'. This is because it gives an immediate sense of both achievement and superiority. The tragedy is that so many of the more brilliant minds in Western civilisation are trapped into this unconstructive mode. It is not as if there was such an ebullience of creative thinking around that we needed the critical thinkers to keep things from running wild. On the contrary, we need to make a great effort to develop design thinking, constructive thinking and creative thinking. I do not think there is really much chance of our educational establishments doing this.

There is more. Proving the other fellow wrong somehow proves us right. This really did apply with medieval theology but no longer does so today, for the real world is not a constructed theology. In the current idiom if you prove the other fellow wrong and he proves you wrong – you may indeed both be wrong.

Perhaps the most wasteful part of this negative idiom is the destruction of a good idea. An idea may be 90% right and 10% wrong (or inadequate). So what do our great thinkers do? Do they try to put that 10% right? No, they jump on the 10%, show up its inadequacy and then imply that anyone who could have put that forward must be an idiot and it therefore follows that the other 90% was thought up by an idiot and is therefore ridiculous.

It really does not require very much thinking to appreciate both the foolishness and the appeal of the clash system. That it should exist somewhere in our thinking culture is valuable; that it should dominate that culture is absurd.

Of course, in attacking this idiom I, myself, have been indulging in negative thinking. That may be because it is necessary to attack an idiom with its own weapons (attack itself being one of those).

'Exlectics'

Now we come to the constructive part. If clash and dialectics are wasteful and dangerous what could we have instead? 'Exlectics' is the alternative mode. It has to do with map reading. It has to do with creative design. The idiom is constructive rather than destructive. Exlectics seeks to 'lead out' or 'pull out' of the situation what is of value – no matter on which side it is to be found.

It is much more than compromise or consensus. Compromise is still within the clash system and suggests that both sides give up something in order to gain something. Consensus means staying with that part of a proposal on which everyone is agreed: it is passive and a lowest common denominator type of approach. Exlectics is rather more like the 'osmosis' method used by the Japanese where there are no opposing or varying ideas to begin with. There is joint listening and joint exploration. It is only later that ideas start to emerge. Views begin to gel after many meetings, whereas in the Western system views are carried in to the very first meeting.

Exlectics is not a matter of dealing with 'views' but of dealing with the terrain. This reflects exactly the sort of difference that was to be found between the intelligence trap and the PMI.

The CoRT tools that are used for exlectics are exploratory and mapping tools.

EBS

A debater tries to find the weakness in the opponent's argument. 'EBS' stands for Examine Both Sides, but this examination has an exploratory purpose. What really is the other point of view – not just as it is expressed in argument form but the 'terrain' behind it? The exploration is neutral. In a classroom a pupil may be asked to put forward one point of view and then, at the last moment, switched to putting forward the other point of view. This is not to demonstrate debating facility but to encourage a genuine examination of both sides. Pupils would be encouraged to explore both sides in such a way that from reading the essays you would be unable to tell which point of view was really favoured. Doing an EBS does not preclude the holding of a point of view, a value system or a preference, but this comes *after* the exploration not, before it.

The EBS is one of those attention-directing tools which seems much easier to use than it really is. On the whole a feeble and off-hand attempt is made to examine the other side – for fear that too good an examination might dilute the fervour with which one's own view is held.

Doing an EBS is – up to a point – not unlike doing a thorough reconnaisance of the enemy's territory in wartime. The crucial difference is that with the wartime reconnaisance you are looking for places to bomb or sabotage whereas with the EBS you are examining the territory for a constructive purpose. The weakness of the tool is that it is not easy to sustain this difference of attitude. The neutrality and objectivity of the examination is crucial. What is required is the detachment of the committed map-maker.

For exercise do an EBS on the following situations: nuclear power stations; public transport strikes; censorship of violence on TV; increased government spending; breakfast TV.

ADI

The EBS mapping exercise leads almost directly into the ADI, which stands for Agreement, Disagreement and Irrelevance. The two maps are compared (from the examination of both sides) and the areas of agreement are noted. Next, the areas of disagreement are noted; finally, the areas of irrelevance. It often turns out that this neutral exploration shows that the areas of disagreement may be quite small but appear very much larger in the argument situation because neither side dare concede a point for fear that this will be used against the arguer. At the end of an effective ADI both parties should be able to point directly at the area of disagreement: 'What we are really in disagreement about is this point here.' Since there will usually be quite a lot on which there is agreement, this can be used as a base for trying to design a way around the disagreement. In any case there is a stronger negotiating base.

Isolating the area of disagreement also means that it can be further examined in order to find out how basic the disagreement may be. Whatever the outcome, it is easier to make progress than with the blanket opposition of the adversary system. Even if the fundamental area of disagreement is one of principle or value it becomes easier to design an outcome that might satisfy both sides. For instance, if there is basic agreement that change must come in the end, then the area of disagreement is about the rate of change, method or stages.

The ADI can be done separately by both parties or it can be done as a cooperative undertaking with both parties sitting down together. The best procedure is the cooperative one but this does depend on the mood of the parties. If this is antagonistic it might be better for each party to do the ADI on its own. Even if the other party is unwilling to do it, there is nothing to stop one party doing it and then presenting it to the other party for modification.

A girl of 15 wants to smoke. She and her father have an argument. The ADI works out something as follows.

Agreement
o the father has a right to his point of view, so does the girl
o that smoking is held to be harmful to the health, now and later
o that many girls of this age do smoke
o that the father has a right to forbid smoking in his house
o that smoking is expensive
o that now or later the girl will eventually have to make her own decision.

Disagreement
o whether father has a right to make his daughter's decisions for her just because she lives in his house
o whether there is any harm in just smoking a few a day
o whether what is at stake is cigarette smoking as such or the girl's independence
o whether if the girl does not smoke now she may never want to smoke.

Irrelevance
o that Susie's father lets her smoke
o that the father has banned some other things

- that the father himself smokes
- that smokers do not harm anyone else
- that the girl could be made into a rebel
- that the girl would smoke secretly anyway.

For exercise, do an imaginary ADI on the following situations: to remain competitive a company wants to introduce partial automation into the factory, the unions oppose this; a boy wants to go to work immediately after leaving school, his father and mother think he should take the chance of going to university; mother wants a stay-at-home holiday, father wants to go abroad; one member of OPEC wants to reduce the price of oil, the others want to maintain it.

'Logic-bubbles'

If someone does not agree with you or does not do what you think he ought to do there are several possible attitudes. He is stupid. He is bloody-minded. He is obstinate. There is, however, an alternative attitude: he is highly intelligent and acting intelligently within his own logic-bubble. And his logic-bubble happens to be different from yours. As suggested in the figure below, a logic-bubble is that bubble of perception within which a person is acting. The bubble includes perception of circumstance, structure, context and relationships.

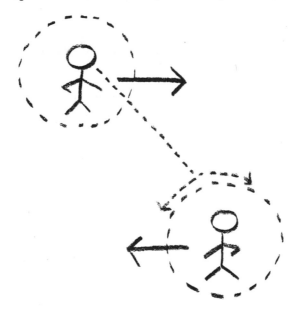

Too often we put intelligent people into certain situations and then complain when they act intelligently. For instance, let us look at innovation in any type of large bureaucracy. If a person tries something and it is a failure, then that failure hangs around his neck for the rest of his career. He cannot recover from it with a following success as he might in business. If his innovation works then he is condemned for not having thought of it sooner or implemented it earlier. If it works he risks being regarded as an 'ideas man' – which means that although this idea has indeed worked, other ideas may not work. When it comes to appointing the head of a department a 'sound' man is to be preferred over an 'ideas' man. For all these reasons innovation is not intelligent behaviour – but survival is. So one can hardly blame a person for acting logically within that particular logic-bubble.

A company has been having a lot of wild-cat strikes. Once the idea of a strike is suggested then the workers do not want to let their mates down, so the strike takes place. The company institutes a small payment for every week of work completed without any such strike. The amount is small when compared to the weekly wage. The strikes diminish to one sixth of what they have been. Is this bribery? It is really a change in the logic-bubble at the moment a strike is suggested. Instead of just following along there is now some reason for a worker to ask 'why?'. Although he may be as ready as ever to go on strike, this slight change at the moment of decision alters his intelligent behaviour through altering the logic-bubble.

It is probably quite far from the truth that everyone is acting very logically within his or her logic-bubble. But as a practical way of looking at things the method has the merit of directing attention not to the stupidity of the person (which is difficult to alter) but to the circumstances (which are easier to alter) in which the behaviour is quite logical.

The logic-bubble includes both the actual circumstances surrounding a person and also his 'perception' of the situation. For example, there may be an actual reward for certain behaviour but this could be perceived as a bribe.

In a company where I had been called in as a consultant to advise on how to make the executives more opportunity conscious, I suggested the setting up of a risk fund which executives could use to finance opportunities – instead of having to divert their operating budgets. One executive said that he did not want to 'risk' using the risk fund because he knew that he would be judged on how he used it. In other words his logic-bubble took into account the risk-averse culture of the company, so the very purpose of the risk fund was negated. He did admit, however, that the mere existence of this fund had allowed him to look at new areas which he was now pursuing as opportunities – but using his own budget.

In any situation it is useful to map out the logic-bubbles of the other people involved. This is especially important in the area of motivation. Management always regards motivation as vital, but motivation depends on the logic-bubble of those who are to be motivated, not on the logic-bubble of management. The same is true for change. The person suggesting the change is convinced of its value, but the people who are going to have to carry through the change have their own logic-bubbles and change usually means risk and hassle and a change in status.

As an exercise, spell out the logic-bubbles of the people involved in the following situations: a naval officer who thinks that his superior has given him a wrong command and a collision is possible; a gossip columnist who has come across a good story involving a friend of hers; Darwin when Alfred Russell Wallace submitted exactly the theory of evolution which Darwin had been working on for years.

OPV

The OPV is another of the CoRT tools. It overlaps with both the EBS and the logic-bubble. It is a simpler and more convenient tool for directing attention to the other people involved in a situation. The letters 'OPV' stand for Other People's Views. In using the tool the thinker tries to put himself in the other person's shoes in order to look at the world from that position.

There are two parts to the exercise. The first part involves the identification of the other people who are really part of the situation. The second part involves getting into the 'shoes' of all these other people. For example, there is a rise in the price of basic farm produce. Do an OPV on this. The first part involves identifying such parties as farmers, wholesalers, retailers, food processors, food buyers, housewives, people in general, economists, government, etc. Then it is a matter of getting inside the thinking of each of these. For example, the retailer may be pleased because if he keeps his usual multiple of buying price for his selling price he will get more money. On the other hand, if people buy less or shift to another sort of food he may lose out. Food processors may suffer because of the increased price of the food they have to buy. On the other hand if people shift from fresh food to cheaper processed food the processor may benefit.

A toy company situated in a country town finds that it can only compete against imported toys if the prices of its products are kept within strict limits. The cost of living is pushing up wages, and the workers ask for a wage rise in line with what workers in other industries are getting. The union supports this claim. An OPV might read as follows:

Owners
o If the plant has to be run at a loss it will be closed down.
o Management should be more productive and find new products.
o Money invested in property or government bonds would give a better rate of return.

Manager
o If the plant closes he will also be without work.
o For the owner to ask for new products is easier said than done, and what if they also meet price competition?
o For the owner to ask for productivity increases is also easier said than done and the last productivity drive has exhausted most possibilities.
o The workers must face the reality of the situation – either the factory stays in business or it does not.

Workers
o They need to live like everybody else – food and other costs have risen with inflation. A wage rise is essential.

- o Profit margins should be cut for the time being.
- o Management should do a better job of marketing and product design.
- o The government should tax imports from cheap labour countries.

Union officials
- o They are elected to represent the workers and must see they get a fair deal.
- o An exception to proper wage rates in this one factory could spread across other factories and erode wages in general.
- o The owner has a social responsibility since his workers helped him build up the business.
- o Management should do a better job.
- o Money can be borrowed to tide them over the difficult times.

Families
- o More money is needed to feed the family.
- o Is it really a toss-up between less money or no job at all?
- o Is it time to start looking for a job elsewhere?
- o Are things going to get better, or worse?
- o Why don't the unions do a better job?
- o A fair wage is due for a fair day's work.
- o Is the threat of closure real or just a threat?
- o The government should do something about cheap imports.

A fuller OPV might extend to the government (and protectionism), toy consumers in general, toy manufacturers and importers, Third World producers and so on.

Doing an OPV does *not* mean putting into the mouths of all parties sane and rational arguments of the sort one might hold oneself. Nor does it mean putting into their mouths complaints and irrationality in order to condemn their point of view. It means objectively trying to look at the world from that point of view – and perhaps adding what is thought to be the actual point of view. In other words it is a blend between the 'position' point of view and the 'actual' point of view (for example, as a reporter might find it).

Unlike the APC (which was covered in an earlier section) the OPV does not involve just giving alternative points of view in general. The emphasis is first of all on specific people in specific positions and then a shift to their points of view.

For exercise do an OPV on the following:

A child is dismissed from school for bullying.
A women accuses her employers of discriminating against her because she is a woman.
A government official wants to retract a confidential piece of information he gave to a reporter.
The sales manager of a publicly owned company is told that bribery is essential for doing business in a particular country.

Constructive design

The mapping techniques mentioned in this section (EBS, ADI, logic-bubble, OPV) are intended to give a broader and clearer view of the situation: a better map. That, in itself, can have a considerable value. If the map is clearer and more complete it is easier to find one's way around.

It may be that the map will reveal that the other party is not interested in solving the dispute at all since the very existence of the dispute is of value to him or her. The way out might then be to allow the dispute to continue at a ritual or cosmetic level whilst the real issues were resolved in a constructive manner.

Where necessary, the second part of the 'exclectic' process might be the constructive design of an outcome or course of action. In a sense this is a 'solution' but that word puts too much emphasis on finding a solution whereas what may be found is a way of living or a way of getting on with things.

In this regard 'constructive design' is no different from constructive design in any other area: furniture, aircraft, TV play or a meal. What are the ingredients? What is to be achieved? What are the priorities? What are the values? What are the channels of action? What are the constraints? The design process may go through several stages, several alternative approaches and several rejections. As in any other area a design is judged to be satisfactory when it is judged to be satisfactory by those who are to use it.

Negotiation

In its true sense negotiation is a specialised form of the constructive design mentioned above. In its 'pressure bargaining' sense it is a form of the clash system.

True negotiation involves thorough mapping of the areas as suggested in this section and then a stage of constructive design.

An important part of negotiation is what might be called 'variable value'.

In Wellington in New Zealand the best hotel in town is built on a site that was acquired for a few thousand dollars. The true value of a site for such an hotel in Wellington would be nearer hundreds of thousands of dollars – even millions. Variable value was involved. The hotel was not built on the ground. It was built on top of a municipal car park. The air rights over the car park were purchased. The value of these air rights to the car park was minimal – in any case the hotel guests and customers would add revenue. The value of the air rights to the hotel builders was great. A classic case of variable value. At the end of the fashion season, dresses in a high-fashion boutique have no re-sale value since that boutique dare not sell last season's styles. But in another store in another part of the country, where fashion took longer to penetrate, those dresses would regain some of their value. Mdina glass, which is made in Malta, is particularly beautiful. Laboratory glass has to be of a very pure quality so as not to contaminate the experiments. Two enterprising people bought up broken laboratory glass in the UK (and were probably paid for taking it away) and converted it into Mdina glass.

All these examples of variable value illustrate that value can differ much according to the person and the situation. That is why it is so central to negotiation. What one party wants very much may cost the other party little. There is a trading in values. There is also a trade-off. In order to drive at reasonable speeds along the road we accept a certain risk of death and injury. To achieve one we have to accept the other. So in negotiation in order to achieve one thing there may have to be acceptance of another.

All this is very much helped by thorough mapping and the attitude of constructive design. Values – and especially perceived values – are the most important ingredient in the design.

Communication

Useful communication must always be in the language of the receiver – which is why legal documents are so unintelligible. The mapping methods listed in this section should be used not only to map out the terrain in terms of position, history, mood and values but also in terms of concepts available.

It is the privilege of the receiver to determine the language that is to be used. It is exactly opposite to radio communication, where it is up to you to tune in your set to whatever is being broadcast.

The logic-bubble of the listener includes the concepts and perceptions available to him or her. It is a bad mistake of communicators to assume that in the absence of a sophisticated concept repertoire (meaning one unlike that of the communicator) all that is left are crude emotions. Simple concepts, such as those held by children, may be very complicated and subtle. Indeed, a simple concept may be more subtle than a complicated one. Complex concepts are often broken down into sub-concepts, whereas simple concepts have to embrace a great deal within one concept. Contrast, for example a child's concept of cause and effect with a scientist's concept which is very much simpler (statistical probability of correlation over time). Adults always tend to think that children have simple adult concepts: but children have complicated child concepts.

Emotions and values

In the end all thinking is emotional. And so it should be.

In the end our decisions, choices and courses of action are all determined by emotions, feelings and values. The purpose of thinking is to serve us as human beings, and feelings are the best judge of the effectiveness of that service.

There is, however, an important point. Do we use emotions first and allow these to determine our perception and our thinking? Or do we use our perception first and allow emotions to determine our final decision?

Gut feeling and thinking

There is amongst some people a belief that thinking is a waste of time and that gut-feeling is all that matters. There is disillusionment with thinking. Thinking seems to be a matter of solving puzzles or playing intellectual word games which are of great interest to philosophers and more or less useless to the real world. Time and again thinking has been seen to rationalise and justify courses of action that have, in hindsight, been inhumane or disastrous. Thinking, like mathematics, is seen as a tool that serves big business and the military as much as it serves anyone else. The thinking of politicians is seen as justifying their continuation in power rather than the improvement of society. Gut feelings and human values are seen to be more reliable.

Much of this disillusionment is directed at the 'intellectualising' type of thinking that seems to exist for its own sake. This is the type of thinking that I described in the 'intelligence trap', where thought is used to justify any position. This is the type of thinking that is used in endless debate and argument and point scoring. This is the type of thinking that is used in philosophical word games. Like everyone else I, also, am disillusioned with that type of thinking. It has its value but as a small part of thinking. Most of thinking needs to be of the common-sense, robust, everyday type of thinking on one level and objective thinking directed towards effectiveness on another.

There is nothing wrong with gut feelings and emotions as the final judges of options. The danger arises if we place them first and use them as a substitute for thinking. To the person holding them at the moment gut feelings always seem true and honest and, by definition, good for society. We must not forget, however, that some of the most ridiculous and inhuman behaviour in the history of man has also been fuelled by gut feelings. Persecutions and wars and lynchings and South Sea bubbles are all a result of gut feeling. No doubt our gut feelings have improved along with the rest of our civilisation, but to entrust them with the task of doing our thinking for us seems, to me, to be too dangerous and too unreliable. For one thing gut feeling seems to favour violence in clash and revolution. Maybe that part of our brain still adheres to the simple methodology of animals.

So I am all in favour of using gut feeling at the end of our thinking but not as a substitute for it. I would also like to insert a 'sense of humour' as one of our gut feelings as otherwise they are always so solemn.

As I see it, the purpose of thinking is so to arrange our view of the world that in the end our emotions can be applied in a fruitful manner.

There is, of course, another reason for our flight from thinking to gut feeling, the stars, and other determinants of action. It is that the world is getting so complicated that it seems impossible to think about anyway. If all the learned economists argue about inflation to the point that the onlooker can only assume they know very little about it, then how is the voter, himself, going to figure out the economic basis for his vote? This is a more serious problem than the first one and seems to demand a much greater attention to the teaching of thinking as a skill in education and elsewhere (even to economists).

Emotions at three points

The figure below shows three possible ways in which emotion can interact with perception. I shall use the word 'perception' rather than thinking for throughout this book I have tried to emphasise that for most practical matters perception is thinking.

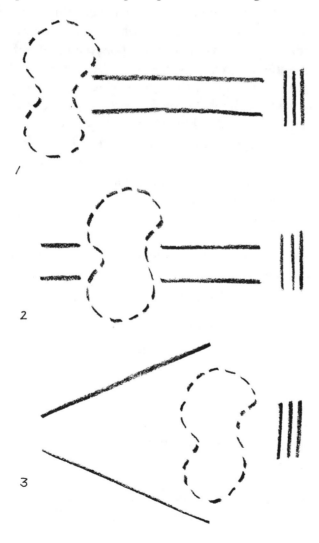

In the first situation the emotion is present from the beginning — even before the particular situation is encountered. This is equivalent to *blind* rage or panic. It may also occur in a particular context even before the details of the situation have been seen. This may happen with aggression, jealousy or hatred. We can call this 'blind emotion'.

The second situation is by far the most usual one. With our perception we examine the situation briefly. We recognise some pattern. That switches on our emotion. From then on our further perception is narrowed and channelled by that emotion. If you offer a foul-looking liquid to people to drink, most of them will wrinkle their noses and decline the offer. A blindfolded person will taste the drink and declare it to be orange juice — which is what it has been all along. The initial perception has triggered our feelings, which then determine our actions.

In the third situation we have the ideal. There is a broad and calm exploration of the situation and in the end emotions come in to make the final decision and choose the course of action. This is the model I have been advocating in this book. Explore first with such tools as PMI, CAF, APC, EBS, ADI, OPV. Then make a choice or decision. This choice may be based on survival, ego-needs, achievement, or self-interest of any sort. These are all emotionally based.

Some years ago a friend of mine stopped to help a lady who had been hit by a motorist and left bleeding at the side of the road. As he was bending over the lady another motorist pulled up and slugged my friend, knocking him unconscious. What had happened was that the motorist's initial perception had interpreted that my friend had knocked the lady down. This triggered his emotions and he reacted accordingly.

The point is a very important one indeed. In general when we think we are acting from gut feeling we nevertheless have a short perception phase during which we interpret the situation. We need to extend that phase and to do far more thinking in it.

There is much less we can do about the 'blind emotion' situation. Jealousy is a most curious emotion since it seems (unlike the other emotions) to have no intrinsic survival value unless on a sexual basis. A person who is jealous of another person will interpret any action whatsoever in a negative manner. As an emotion jealousy is more interesting than most and could benefit from some scrutiny.

Changing feelings

But can perceptions change feelings? Many believe that perception or thinking cannot really change feeling. The orange juice experiment is a suggestion that such change is impossible. Consider a man who is having an argument with a woman who is in tears. The man feels that he is a bully and is about to concede some points – then a friend whispers to him that he is being emotionally blackmailed. At once his attitude changes. This suggestion has changed his perception or way of looking at things – and with this his feelings. A woman feels that she has to look after her ageing parents and cannot therefore get married. A friend tells her that she is making herself a 'victim' and at once her attitude and feelings change.

David Lane used the CoRT thinking lessons at the Hungerford Guidance Centre and told me the effect they had on the violent youngsters. Before the lessons the youngsters had been inclined to react with a violent cliché when asked to think about society or their place in it. The question triggered their emotions and the reaction followed. After the thinking lessons they had developed some pride in themselves as 'thinkers'. There was now a thinking pause instead of a rush to reaction. There was more consideration and more objectivity to the thinking. Edna and Bill Copley reported a similar trend when using the CoRT lessons in a borstal institution.

It is possible for thinking to alter feelings – especially the perceptual type of thinking which allows us to see things in a different way. The PMI demonstration I mentioned earlier in the book showed how some simple thinking changed the feelings of children who had at first welcomed the idea of being paid to go to school.

We shall see later in this section how certain 'value-laden' words can alter perceptions and feelings. Some new proposal is put to a work force to settle an industrial dispute. At first they are inclined to accept it – then it becomes labelled as a bribe or a trick and feelings begin to change.

Values

Values are the link between events and our basic emotions. They are converters which convert events into matters about which we can feel strongly. Values are the most important ingredient in civilisation. It is by means of values that civilisation turns selfish, greedy, aggressive, short-term behaviour into social cooperation which makes life better for everyone and cares for the weak. The astonishing power of values to reverse normal human feelings is shown by Christianity. Martyrs suffered pain and willingly gave up their lives for the greater glory of God. Suffering itself had a value. Enemies were to be loved. Compassion was to be shown to the poor. In all these cases the value system succeeded in converting one lot of emotions into another.

For convenience we might look at four types of values – the '4M' system.

Me-values: ego, status, self-importance, achievement, survival, pleasure, self-indulgence, etc.

Mates-values: being accepted by the group, belonging to the group, acting as a member of the group, accepting the values of the group, not letting the group down.

Moral-values: religious values, social custom, general observance of the law, upbringing values, general values of a particular culture (often regarded as absolute but varying much from culture to culture).

Mankind-values: (relatively new) ecology, pollution, concern with nuclear power, a general concern for the whole earth and mankind upon it, also human rights and a concern for basic human values that transcend cultures.

HV and LV

It is a useful attention directing technique to attempt to divide the values occurring in any situation into 'High Values' and 'Low

Values'. This is one of the CoRT lessons. In general the high values are the ones which determine action and the low values are the ones which have to be taken into account. Imagine a cost squeeze in an industrial company. There is to be a reduction in staff. The head of one division is being pressured to get rid of an assistant who has been with him for fifteen years. What are the values involved? This could read as follows.

HV: fear that he, the division head, could lose his own job if he did not comply; fear of the company collapsing; fear that he would not get promotion; loyalty to his assistant; the ego need to be successful and to be seen to be successful.

LV: the awkwardness of sacking the man; fear of what people might say; dislike of his own boss; the cost of compensation; the effect on other workers.

The exercise is a difficult one. For example, in the above situation loyalty to his subordinate might have been classed as either a low or high value. It might be valued highly but in the work context would easily be over-ridden by other values, since 'efficiency' would be seen to be the value in that context.

In fact the exercise is based on the 'apple-sorting' story. A French farmer goes off to market in the morning. He asks his two sons to sort a huge pile of apples into big apples and small apples while he is gone. They work all day to do this, carefully assessing whether a particular apple is big or small. The farmer returns and mixes both piles of apples together again. The sons are furious at having wasted their time. But the farmer points out that the real object of the exercise was to get 'full attention' paid to the apples so that the *bad* ones would be thrown out – as indeed they have been. The 'big versus small' discrimination requires much more careful scrutiny than just looking for the bad apples. So the HV and LV exercise is really an instruction to look very carefully at the values involved in any situation.

Teacher has forbidden the eating of sweets in the classroom. A boy notices that his neighbour is eating sweets – should he sneak on him?
What if there is a broken window and the boy knows the culprit?

o What if there has been a lot of stealing and the boy knows who the thief is?

o What if it is a police state and your neighbour is giving refuge to a dissident wanted by the police?

o What if there is hunger in the country and your neighbour is hoarding food?

o What if you are informing on a terrorist gang?

o What if you are a member of a gang and inform on them?

o What if you are a paid police informer?

o What if you secretly and anonymously tell tales on your friends to gossip columnists?

It is most interesting to see how, in a roomful of people, the process of 'sneaking or informing' becomes respectable at one moment and shameful at another. This is a very sensitive example of the clash of values. It is also a good example of the importance of context and hypocrisy. If we dislike another regime (probably justifiably) then any sort of sneaking in that regime is abhorrent. If it is our own society then there are times when informing is not only respectable but a social duty. Similarly we would not like the idea of people sneaking on their friends, especially if we are involved, but at the same time we enjoy reading the results of that sneaking. The situation is an interesting one because of the constant clash between me-values, mates-values and moral-values.

Value-laden words

The very words 'sneak' and 'informer' carry a heavy negative value. A great number of the words we use have such values.

I would go so far as to say that more than three-quarters of our public thinking is no more than an attempt to drag in value-laden words as soon as we possibly can. And then to rest the argument on those words.

If you read the average newspaper editorial or listen to the average political speech you may find that it is no more than a thin net of rational argument supporting a heavy burden of value-laden words.

There are the 'goodie' words such as: moral debt, justice, honour, fair play, freedom, press freedom, consistency, human rights, sincere, direct, perceptive, etc.

Then there are the 'baddie' words, which are much more numerous: obstinate, stubborn, sly, cunning, clever, deceitful, well-meaning, misguided, egotist, manipulative, self-seeking, publicity seeking, populariser, superficial, capitalist, socialist, small-minded, shifty etc. These are quite apart from the directly negative words like 'foolish' or 'incompetent' which are honest judgements. The danger is much more with the sneer words which slip by and yet carry their value with them. A good example is the phrase 'well-intentioned' which sounds positive but is used in a negative way.

The following passage is taken from a piece which describes the value of the charismatic movement to the development of Christianity.

'The openness of Christianity to development and growth has maintained a creative tension that keeps faith lively.'

The words 'openness', 'development', 'growth', 'creative' and 'lively' are all value-laden words with an upbeat effect.

In California I once had a discussion with a psychologist in which I was taking a provocative position by asserting that the whole post-Freudian emphasis on digging deeper to find the 'true self' and the 'real cause of behaviour' might be going in the wrong direction. I was suggesting that perhaps it was the surface personality that mattered, the mask which a person constructed for himself or herself to wear to face the world. The interesting thing was that the discussion was almost impossible because all the words I used had an intrinsic negative value: surface, superficial, mask, constructed, veneer. All the words he used had an in-built positive value: true self, underlying nature, real self, deep truth, mainspring of action, and hidden causes. This is because we have assigned these values from within the Freudian idiom itself (so used are we to it).

Exactly the same thing happens if you try to discuss placing an employee in a position where he will not only be happy but will do his best work. All the words you use will end up sounding like 'manipulation' which, rightly, has a negative content. Even if you let the employee do his own choosing or even designing his own job the connotation is that you are doing it for your good, not his, and therefore it is manipulation.

It is frightening to see how many subjects cannot be discussed because the very words we need to use have been so contaminated with in-built values that whatever we say is pre-judged. If you try to explain something complex in a simple way you are a 'populariser', which is a most convenient, all-embracing sneer word.

As an exercise it is useful to go through a political speech or newspaper editorial (or even better newspaper letters) and circle with a marker all the value-laden words that are used. The end result surprises most people.

Amongst the value-laden words should also be mentioned those words which have the special value of sounding important and saying very little: 'concerned about', 'pay attention to this', 'have at heart', 'will look into', 'some progress'. They are mainly political words which are used to say a lot when no real promise or commitment can be made.

Awareness

The examination of values is an awareness exercise. It is a matter of becoming aware of the values that are inherent in a situation, the conflict of values, the values that are perceived by the people involved and the source of these values. Consider the values involved in the following situations: an inventor who designs a loom that is three times as fast as existing ones; an employee who knows that his boss takes bribes but also knows that the boss has a very high regard for the employee; public transport strikes; a doctor who charges very high fees for a life-saving operation; a government that abolishes patents on drugs within its borders; a politician who deserts his party and moves to a new party.

The most important exercise of all is the one suggested above: an examination of written, or spoken, material in order to pull out the value-laden words. It is surprising to see how much of what passes for thinking is no more than a skilful necklace of value-laden words.

Making decisions

Making decisions is always a practical matter and I intend to deal with the subject in that way.

The size of a decision is always proportional to the inadequacy of the reason for making it.

If information is sufficient to make the decision for us then we, as humans, are superfluous. We are only called in to make decisions when an analysis of information is insufficient – that is to say, when we have to speculate or guess or apply human values and emotions. So the human element in decisions is vital. In the end all decisions are emotional.

I am therefore going to deal with quite ordinary decisions – not the sort that would require running various factors through an econometric model. In the end even such decisions end up as ordinary human decisions.

The figure overleaf shows a particular state of play in the L-Game. One of the players can win in one move. As mentioned earlier, the rules of the game are that each player has an L-piece which can be moved to any vacant position. Following that a player can, if he wishes, move either one of the small neutral pieces to any new position. The object of the game is to block the opponent's L-piece so that there is no position to which it can be moved.

The type of decision needed for the L-Game play is a simple one

because the value of the decision can be checked: it wins the game or it does not. In almost all decision situations the difficulty is that the value of the decision can only be checked in the future – after the decision has been made. The L-Game play may require a search through a large number of alternatives, but again these are limited in number. In other decisions the number of alternatives is only limited by our imagination.

Decision pre-frame

This is the setting for the decision. What is the context? What is the situation in which the decision is to be made: calm, panic, conflict, competitive pressure, or what? Why is there a need to make a decision at all? Why is there a need to make it now? If the decision is put off will the matter resolve itself or will an opportunity be lost? Is there pressure to make the decision? Is this pressure self-imposed, imposed by others or imposed by the advice of friends?

What is the time scale of the decision? This applies both to the making of the decision and also to the effects. Does the decision have to be made today, this month, this year, within the next decade? When will the effects of the decision become apparent, next week or in twenty years' time (as with buying new electric power stations)?

Finally there is the 'type' of decision. Is it an adjustment or change in direction, or is it a major switch? Is it a decision to stop doing something or to start doing something? Is it the sort of decision that depends very much on other people for its implementation or is it one that can be made directly by the deciders? Is it irrevocable or can it be reversed if it does not work out? Is it one among many decisions or one which sets the course for all that follows? Is it a decision that the people making the decision are capable of making?

We can summarise all these as: context, need, time scale and type.

Generation of alternatives

There are some obvious alternatives and some that have to be discovered – or designed – by creative thought. At least some conscious effort needs to be made to generate alternatives beyond the obvious ones. There must, however, be a practical cut-off when a decision has to be made. To hope for the ultimate alternative is unrealistic. This need to generate alternatives was covered at length in an earlier section so there is no point in repeating it here. It is enough to say that when a decision is difficult to make it is always worth going back to try to generate further alternatives.

Values and priorities

These can be spelled out in advance. Priorities may sometimes appear as values and sometimes as sub-objectives (things that one wants to achieve). Values and priorities are interwoven in the ten decision methods which follow.

The dice method

List the alternatives and just throw a dice to decide which one is to be followed. Although this seems bizarre, irrational and impossible to do, there is quite a lot of sense to it. The burden of the decision is placed on 'someone else'. In this case it is a die – in other cases it may be the stars, a fortune teller, fate, etc. The underlying point is a simple one.

Is it more important to make the right decision or to be happy with the decision you have made?

Psychologists have long known that people tend to get to like and to justify decisions after they have been made. So there is logic to the dice method: make the decision and then get to like the result.

The dice method is suggested as a serious method because in some situations 'making a decision work' is even more important than choosing the right decision.

A rich uncle offers you a choice of the following for your birthday:

1 A new pair of shoes
2 A visit to the theatre
3 A meal in a restaurant with friends of your choice
4 Six books (or tapes) of your choice
5 A Rolls-Royce for three hours
6 An instant picture camera.

As an exercise toss a die, see which number comes up, and see if you would be happy with that decision.

The easy way out method

In the end decisions not only have to be made but they also have to be acted upon. Clearly some alternatives are much easier to choose and to act upon than others. The 'easy way out' method places the emphasis on this. What is the easiest alternative to choose? This may, of course, vary from one personality to another so the choice is subjective. Once this choice of the easy way out has been made, then the effort is made to build up and justify this decision. This is a *conscious, positive* effort. If at the end of this effort the choice now seems an acceptable one it can be made. If it still does not seem acceptable then some other decision method is needed.

A girl finds that her boy-friend has asked her best friend to go out with him. She has the following alternatives.

1 Ignore it completely.
2 Ask him about it.
3 Have a row with him.
4 Warn her friend off.
5 Go out with someone else.

The 'easy way out' would depend much on personality, and a different personality might regard any of these as the easy way out. Choosing the easy way out is the first step: if that choice can be justified – so much the better.

The spell-out method

Here the decider imagines that he has chosen each alternative in turn. In each case he imagines that he is describing to a friend why he has made that decision. In this imaginary scenario he puts forward all the reasons why it is a good choice and why it suits him. Each of these justifications should be written down and then read through in their own right. Which one sounds the best? Which one makes the most sense? The best one may sometimes stand out very clearly. At other times some of the justifications are so feeble that those alternatives disappear from the list.

Office workers in an insurance company are offered the following choice of incentives:

1. More money
2. A shorter working week
3. Longer holidays
4. More time off when required.

The choices are to be made by individuals. Imagine you are one of those individuals. Go through each of the alternatives and imagine that you had chosen that alternative, imagine you were justifying that particular choice to a friend. Because the justifications will vary with personal situations use your own situation (family size, etc).

The 'spell-out' method is an extension of the 'easy way out' method, only this time each alternative gets the justification treatment. The more formal the spelling-out of the reasons, the more successful will the method be.

Balaam's ass method

Balaam's ass is more usually known as Buriden's ass, but the behaviour is the same. This mythical ass was placed at exactly the mid-point between two exactly equal bundles of hay. The ass starved to death because at no instant could it decide which bundle of hay to approach. The balance was so exactly equal that the ass was immobilised. This poor ass was much used by philosophers in their endless discussions about free-will when such discussions were fashionable.

In terms of decisions the point made by the ass is an important one. When the alternatives are all equally attractive it should be the easiest decision ever, because whichever choice is made will be agreeable. It would only be a matter of tossing a coin and being happy with the result (dice method application). Why then are such decisions so very difficult — as with a young lady trying to decide which of two eligible bachelors she should wed? The answer must be that the difficulty lies in bringing ourselves to *give up* an attractive alternative. In other words, the problem with the ass was his reluctance to turn his back on either lovely bundle of hay. Once we know we are going to have something then the attraction of that fades but the anguish of giving up something else grows.

The Balaam's ass method tackles this problem directly. The decision maker does his very best to 'knock' or make unattractive each alternative in turn. If he succeeds then there is no pain in giving them up and the best decision emerges.

Suppose a magic jinn appeared and offered you a to-be-granted wish. There was to be the following choice:

1   to be very wise
2   to be very rich
3   to be very beautiful
4   to be a talented artist.

The knocking could take the following form:

1   To be very wise: you might find everyone else foolish; you might be more aware of the misery of the world.
2   To be very rich: you would never know who your friends were; you might become jealous of others who were richer; you would have many worries.

3 To be very beautiful: you would worry about losing your beauty; you would attract unsavoury characters; you would become spoiled.
4 To be a talented artist: very frustrating if nobody recognised your talent; there would always be new horizons; talent can be a burden.

The final choice is still a matter of personal opinion but it has now become easier to give up the alternatives that are not chosen.

The ideal solution method

In this method the alternatives are listed – and then ignored. Instead an 'ideal solution' is fashioned for the situation. The general 'shape' of this ideal solution is considered. It should not be detailed but the characteristics should be noted. The list of alternatives is now uncovered and examined to see which of them approaches the nearest to the 'ideal solution'. In other words, the alternatives are no longer examined in their own right but for their nearness to the 'ideal'.

A small town has a vacant lot and the following suggestions are made for the use of that lot:

1 Car park
2 More houses
3 Park
4 Playground
5 Open (stall-type) market.

These alternatives are put on one side and there is a discussion about the general shape of the ideal solution. It is agreed that this should benefit most people and that it should directly make life more pleasant. When the actual alternatives are compared to this 'ideal solution' the park alternative wins. In using this method it is important to be honest and not just to fashion the 'ideal solution' to fit one or other of the known alternatives. For the same reason it does not make sense to design the ideal solution first and then to list the alternatives because these will be fashioned to meet that solution. Such fashioning can take place later. The first list of alternatives should be an objective one – before the ideal solution is shaped.

The best home method

The best 'home' for an idea is that situation or context in which the idea would thrive. Just as in a room there may be the best setting for a vase of flowers or in a football team there may be the best position for a certain player, so we can describe the best setting or 'home' for a particular idea. In this case the ideas are the alternatives that are offered for the decision. For each alternative we find the best home. For what type of person in what type of circumstance would that choice of alternative be the best? For example, if someone was very rude to you and you had two alternatives (for the sake of the example) one of which was to punch the fellow, then the best home for this alternative would be someone with a fiery temper and enough muscle. You then compare that 'home' to actuality: are you a fiery person of brawn?

A small manufacturing company sets out to make electric light bulbs. A choice of strategy is discussed, with the following two alternatives emerging:

1   Make bulbs that are cheaper than everyone else's but do not last as long.
2   Make super bulbs that last longer but must be sold at a higher price.

The best home for the cheaper bulbs idea is a large company with economies of scale, a good advertising budget, a good distribution system and the ability to shift prices to match competition. The best home for the super bulb is a small company that needs good profit margins and that can exist on a small or niche share of the market. When the best 'home' is compared to actuality it seems that the super bulb is the better product.

As with some of the other methods, there must be a great deal of objectivity in finding the best 'home' for the alternative.

The 'What if . . . ?' method

Different 'what if . . . ?' type changes are made in the circumstances to see at what point an alternative suddenly stops being attractive.

Suppose you had decided to go to Marbella for a holiday and then generated the following what ifs:

o What if it rained every day?
o What if you did not meet a soul?
o What if Marbella is unfashionable this year?

When you hit on a 'what if' that makes the choice unattractive then you have isolated the real reason behind making that particular choice. In the above example if a degree of 'unfashionableness' made the choice of Marbella lose its appeal, then obviously the feeling of being in fashion is part of the decision process – in which case one might choose a place more fashionable than Marbella.

A husband and wife both have excellent jobs and the children are grown up. The husband is then offered a job he has always wanted in a town two hundred miles away. At the moment it does not seem likely that the wife will be able to find a suitable job in the new place. There are the following alternatives (for the sake of the exercise, because in practice one would generate far more alternatives):

1 Turn down the offer.
2 Accept the offer and meet at weekends.
3 Wife gives up job and moves.
4 Accept it and then resign later if necessary.

We then try the following 'what ifs':

o What if the job is not as attractive as it seems?
o What if whilst separated either party meets someone else?
o What if either party falls ill?
o What if it had been the wife who had the job offer?
o What if a better job in the same place was possible for either?
o What if the wife did find a job in the new place?

The process is really a focusing one.

o Is the job offer really as attractive as it seems?
o Is any job the most important part of life?
o Should the wife make the decision?

The simple matrix method

A matrix is a grid, as shown below. On the side you list the alternatives. Along the top you list the qualities you are looking for. In the boxes you indicate how a particular alternative relates to that particular quality.

	PRICE	RUNNING COST	RELIABILITY
REPAIR			X
NEW CAR	X		
SECOND HAND			
LEASE			
HIRE	X		

In the simple matrix method an attempt is made to pick out the few crucial qualities that would be required for any decision. Without these qualities the decision would not make sense. It is really a way of screening out those alternatives which are totally unsuitable.

For example, an old car fails to pass its roadworthiness test. There seem to be the following alternatives:

1   Spend money on repairing it.
2   Buy a new car.
3   Buy a secondhand car.
4   Lease a car.
5   Hire a car only when required.

The 'crucial' qualities are identified as being: cost of acquiring the car, cost of running the car, convenience and reliability (taken together). The next figure shows what happens in the simple matrix. Some of the alternatives are weeded out — because they do not pass the test. The remaining alternatives can be treated with another decision method, or else a further 'crucial' quality can be tested. This can go on with the application of further qualities until only one alternative survives. In a sense the simple matrix method is a 'survival' method. Which alternatives survive the crucial demands?

The full matrix method

Here the matrix lists *all* the priorities and values and considerations that need to go into the decision. They are all laid out from the beginning, and each alternative is examined to see which qualities it possesses. In the end those alternatives showing the most qualities are looked at again. At this point another decision method could be used. It is rather dangerous simply to take the alternative with the most qualities because the qualities are not of equal importance. The possession of two lesser qualities is not more important than the possession of a major quality (there are ways around this but they are complicated and, in the end, subjective).

The figure below shows a full matrix for a choice between three different styles of kitchen furniture: modern, traditional and functional. The qualities are price, aesthetic appeal, fits in with house, sturdiness, durability, ease of cleaning or repair, convenience and safety. In this case the 'modern' style appears to win. At this point, however, it is still possible to say: 'The modern style is obviously the best buy — but I prefer the look of the traditional.' The decision is now a rational one: aesthetics are more important than anything else to this buyer.

	PRICE	LOOKS	FIT IN	STURDINESS	DURABILITY	CLEANING	SAFETY	
MODERN	✔		✔	✔	✔	✔	✔	6
TRAD.	✔	✔	✔		✔			4
FUNCTIONAL	✔			✔	✔		✔	4

The laziness method

The method is simple and direct and closely related to human nature. Each alternative is examined to see what contribution fear, greed and laziness would make to the choice of that alternative. In other words, what is the real motivating force behind this choice? The method could also be called the 'FGL' method (Fear, Greed, Laziness).

A grandmother has been living on her own. Her son feels that she might be getting too old to continue on her own. He considers the following alternatives:

1   Leave things as they are.
2   Place her in an old people's home.
3   Have her come and live with his family.
4   Pay someone to look after her.

With the first alternative there is a large element of laziness (least effort choice). There is also the fear that something might happen to her. On the greed side it seems less expensive than the others.

Placing the lady in an old people's home has an element of laziness (off his hands). It could be expensive (greed element). There is the fear the old lady might not like it.

Having her come to live with him arouses the fear that she might not get on with his wife and might upset the family. There could be a greed element if she is likely to leave money in her will.

Paying for a housekeeper could be expensive. There is a strong laziness element in the shifting of responsibility to someone else. The fear element is only the fear of what others might say were he to place her in an old people's home.

In the end the decision, like all decisions, will be made emotionally. But the picture is now clearer.

There are times when it may be seen that greed, fear or laziness are the main contributors to the attractiveness of a particular alternative.

Decision post-frame

Personal style and self-image is a very important factor here. Is it the sort of decision that one can see oneself making? If the decision is a ruthless one, can the person making it see himself – or herself – carrying it through? Decisions need to be objective but the personal style of the decider is part of that objectivity.

The people involved need a lot of consideration. They may have to agree to the decision. They may have to carry it through. They may be affected by it. At this point such techniques as the OPV or logic-bubble (mentioned in an earlier section) need to be applied.

The consequences of the decision have to be examined in the different time frames: immediate, short term, medium term and long term (by doing a C & S, as suggested in an earlier section).

Then there is the implementation of the decision. Who is going to implement it? How is it going to be implemented? Are the channels available or must they be set up? What are the stages of implementation? What are the likely problems and sticking points? What are the risks and dangers? All these points apply to any course of action (and will therefore be considered in a later section).

What is the terrain? This is a 'map' of the circumstances or environment in which the decision is going to be carried out. It includes competitors, rivals and the state of the world – both on a large scale and a small scale.

Finally, there is the 'fall-back' position. What if the decision soon proves to be wrong? What if it cannot be implemented? What if circumstances change? Can the decision be reversed? Is rescue possible? Can there be a switch to a reserve position? It sometimes feels as though the design of a fall-back position weakens the confidence with which a decision is made. If you are sure it is the right decision why design an escape route? But all decisions are speculative – otherwise they would not be decisions. There is a difference between being unwilling to take risks and making provision for things not turning out as hoped.

Emphasis on fit

It may have been noticed that in many of the methods suggested the emphasis is not directly on the value of the alternatives but on how they 'fit' the actual circumstances. We need to change difficult decisions into easy decisions first. In the end *all* decisions must be emotional, but the clearer the picture the more suitable the application of the emotions.

Thinking and doing

It is a particularly silly aspect of culture that separates thinkers from doers. Thinkers are not supposed to do. Doers are not supposed to think. Thinking can be used as an excuse for inaction: the preference for the perfect thought over the practical action. Thinkers can await full information and full detail before proceeding to action. Thinkers can so qualify and hedge their suggestions 'on the one hand and on the other hand' that practical action is impossible. From all this arises the 'academic' view of thinking. In American universities the academics are encouraged to spend part of their time in the real world of action. In British universities this is frowned upon. There is, of course, a place for academic intellectualising and passive scholarship (which consists of repeating what others have repeated about still yet others) but that is only a small part of thinking – but valuable nevertheless. Broad, practical, robust and action-directed thinking is not an inferior sort of thinking but in many ways superior. Uncertainties and risks have to be assessed, courses of action have to be 'designed'.

Then there are the 'doers' who claim that very little thinking is needed for doing. If this were so then there are three options: 'seat of the pants', routine or chance. There are times when seat of the pants experience may be sufficient for action, but as soon as competition starts doing some thinking, 'seat of the pants experience' may not know how to respond. Routine is also adequate in a simple non-competitive world. That is why, in the insurance business which has been traditionally run by 'seat of the pants experience' and routine, there has always been a chance for the maverick who does think to come in and make a fortune. Chance is much used under the guise of 'simple common sense'. Those whom chance then favours surface and the many more whom chance does not favour never emerge.

It is perfectly true that the characteristics of 'effectiveness' are more important in doing than intellectual niceties. But the characteristics of effectiveness include a great deal of thinking: especially of the goal-setting variety. The action-directed thinker is perhaps more concerned with the positive aspects of the possible than with doubts and fears, but that is thinking none the less. That a doer should stand up and proclaim his pride in *not* thinking reflects either upon his luck or the poor image that thinking possesses. Over the years I have come into contact with many of the major corporations in Europe, America and the East (IBM, Unilever, Shell, General Dynamics, Marsh McLennan, Bank of America, CSR etc). There is no doubt at all that they put a very high emphasis on thinking. Indeed, I would go so far as to say that business, in general, is far more interested in thinking than any other sector of society – not excluding education.

Operacy

The idiom of education is that it is enough to build up the information base and that action is then easy. It is not. The skills of action are every bit as important as the skills of knowledge. That this is not recognised in education is a tragedy. For convenience I have coined the term 'operacy', which is derived from 'operate' and 'operational' and thus indicates 'the skills needed for doing'. These skills include the thinking skills needed for doing (like setting objectives). As I mentioned earlier, I believe that operacy should rank alongside literacy and numeracy as a major aim of education.

Three ways of doing things

There are three traditional ways of doing things. We can take the model of a ball rolling down a slope, as suggested below.

The first way is shown in the figure below which gives an overhead view of the slope with the ball starting in one corner.

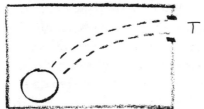

The 'T' stands for the target. We set up a groove or channel for the ball to follow as it moves towards the target. This is equivalent to setting up procedures and routines – a very effective method, even if it lacks flexibility.

The second method:
Here a small electric light bulb is placed at the 'T' position and the ball is equipped with some sensing device which allows it to find its own way towards the target. This is goal-directed behaviour or management by objectives. In order to operate, it needs a 'higher calibre' of person than the first method but is much more flexible since you can start from anywhere and the target can easily be changed.

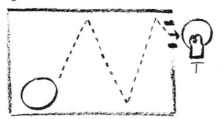

The third method:
Here the ball is simply released. *After* the ball has arrived at the edge of the slope we designate that position as the 'T' or target. In other words we proceed along without a real objective and pretend that where we are is where we set out to reach.

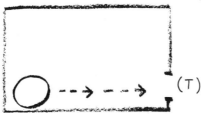

Setting objectives

In the BBC Television series I set the task of moving as many eggs as possible from one place to another within twenty seconds. The instinctive reaction (especially under the time pressure) was for each of the two operators to carry across as many as possible on each trip. The second time around the participants were asked to do some thinking first. Not surprisingly some of them thought in terms of sub-objectives: what needed to be achieved in order to make achieving the ultimate objective easier. There was a suggestion of using an available piece of cloth as a receptacle in which to carry the eggs.

AGO

This is another of the attention-directing 'thinking tools' which is also included in the CoRT thinking lessons. Although the tool is very simple to use, this particular lesson is one of the most difficult in practice. Youngsters find it very hard indeed to think in terms of objectives. This may be because their own lives are so arranged by other people (having to do this and having to do that) that setting an objective is something quite strange. If asked why some action is done they would answer: 'Because I have to.' The idea of setting up an objective (or sub-objective) and then working towards it seems very strange. Since there is no emphasis on operacy, there probably is no point in their education at which this can change. Setting out to pass an exam is really still following the routine channel prescribed by others – it is more an intention than an objective.

'AGO' stands for Aims, Goals and Objectives. Although there are differences between the three words these differences are ignored for the sake of the attention-directing tool. There are circumstances where one or other of the terms would fit best but, in general, the task is to set up objectives or to pick out the objectives that seem to be in use.

For example 'doing an AGO' on the aims of a car designer might turn up the following:
o   fit the market trend and need (looking ahead as well)

- right price bracket
- distinctive advertisable features
- economic to run
- reliable
- eye-catching style

Some of these include other sub-objectives. For example, 'economic to run' includes aerodynamic styling so as to reduce drag. In this regard priorities come to be included as sub-objectives.

For exercise, spell out the AGO in the following situations: setting up an anti-litter campaign; running a city police force; designing a children's game; buying a holiday house; planning a career; choosing a camera; meeting new friends.

Targets

A target is just another term for an objective. As suggested in the figure below, a target may be far or near. It may also be wide or narrow. It follows that if a target is both wide and near then success is more easily assured. So it is not just a matter of saying: 'That is my target, how do I get there?' It is also a matter of designing or changing the target so that it becomes more easily accessible. Dimitri Comino, who invented the very successful Dexion slotted angle strip, once told me how his invention was designed as a target that was both near and wide. The strip had so many uses that even if one market segment did not work out, there were many others.

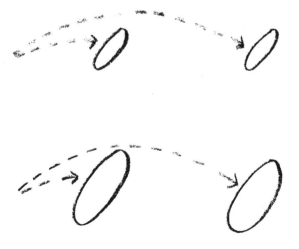

If you are throwing darts at a dartboard and your aim is not very exact, it would be nice if – somehow – the dartboard moved to meet your flying dart so that this landed in the bullseye. It would be nice but rather unlikely. In a similar manner if you manufacture a radio and then hope that the market will 'move' to like it, you may be disappointed. Far better to spend more time on a better aim – finding out what the market really wants.

Strategy and tactics

At several points in this book I have mentioned the L-Game which I once designed as the 'simplest possible real game'. New players find it hard to develop an effective strategy precisely because the game seems so simple. As a broad strategy they might offer the following:

o break up the empty spaces
o stay close to the opponent's L-piece
o use the neutral pieces to block rows and columns
o dominate the centre
o keep out of the corners
o force the opponent to the edge.

All these are general 'guidelines' or broad strategy. Within that broad strategy there are moment-to-moment moves that have to be made. These are the 'tactics'. A computer company might have the broad strategy of 'riding on the coat-tails of IBM'. Within this broad strategy there are many tactical decisions that have to be made: to avoid directly competitive products; to make sensitive pricing decisions; to anticipate IBM policy. Another computer company might adopt the strategy of catering for customers who needed the utmost reliability in their computers rather than the most advanced system. Yet another company might direct its attention to the small business user. This company might use the tactic of making personal computers in order to get people used to its products and then offering rather more powerful machines. In this case it may be difficult to decide whether this is really a 'tactic' or a 'sub-strategy'. The important point is that the strategy is the overall intention and way of behaving which itself guides the moment-to-moment movement or tactics.

Corporate strategy has recently become a much more fashionable subject. This is because in a competitive world it is no longer enough to rely on a dominating market position – or just quick reactive behaviour to whatever a competitor has done.

Courses of action

In the L-Game there are so many possible courses of action at any one moment that it is virtually impossible to work through the consequences of any one move. One way around this is to work 'backwards' from the winning positions. Most of the winning positions (but not all) have the losing L-piece in a corner. So we assume that if the opponent can be forced into a corner we shall eventually block his piece. Then the opponent learns to keep out of the corner. So we must now learn a move which will force the opponent into a corner. He learns that too. So we learn the move that will force him into the position from which we can force him into the corner from whence we can block him. In effect we are 'working backwards'.

We can look at the same process in another way. Suppose we wanted to get to Edinburgh. We then worked backwards from Edinburgh. If only we could get to Newcastle then the next bit to Edinburgh would be easy. So we make Newcastle the objective. Then we find a town from which it would be easy to get to Newcastle – and so on.

This working backwards process is illustrated overleaf.

It is a very powerful way of designing a course of action. In fact it designs several courses of action, and then we look around to see how close we actually are to one of the 'entry points'. It must be said that 'working backwards' is not easy because it requires a great deal of mental effort and the ability to imagine things.

The points from which we could get to the final objective become objectives in themselves and so on as we work backwards. Action is thus divided up into easy stages. It may not be the most efficient method (for example, the road to Edinburgh may bypass Newcastle) but it is an effective one in situations where there are no obvious courses of action.

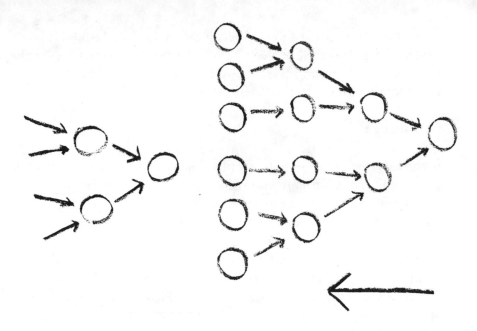

If-box maps

I described the 'if-box map' method in my book *Opportunities*. It is a convenient notation for mapping out a course of action so that we can separate the 'action channels' from the if-boxes.

An 'action channel' is something that we can do as soon as we decide to do it. The channel is there, and there is nothing to stop us advancing along it. For example, if you want to ask a friend to lend you some money there is nothing to stop you picking up the telephone and calling him.

You can call your friend but you do not have any control over whether or not he will lend you the money. The best you can do is to make a good case and exert your sales charm. Since you do not have control this is an 'if-box'. You have to await the outcome. It depends on factors beyond your control. You are held up. You cannot advance as you might along an action channel.

The idea is to plot a course of action by dividing it into 'action channels' (which you can zoom along) and 'if-boxes' (where you are held up).

For example, if you conceived the business idea that it might make sense to set up a camera rental business (in the same way as there exist car rental businesses) for people going on holiday, scenic spots, special occasions, you might construct an if-box map as shown below.

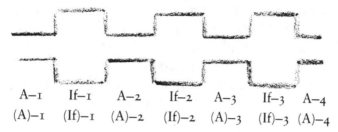

A–1   If–1   A–2   If–2   A–3   If–3   A–4
(A)–1   (If)–1   (A)–2   (If)–2   (A)–3   (If)–3   (A)–4

The letters below refer to the letters on the map.

A–1   Approach a bank for finance
If–1   If the bank agrees to lend money
A–2   Pay for a market survey
If–2   If the survey shows there is a market
A–3   Approach camera company for special deal
If–3   If camera company agrees to such a deal
A–4   Look for premises, etc.

We might look at the above if-box map and decide that it does not offer the best sequence of action channels and if-boxes. So we might set up our map as follows:

(A)–1   Look for a shop at a holiday resort
(If)–1   If you find one
(A)–2   Rent the shop for a season
(If)–2   If your trial of renting cameras succeeds
(A)–3   Approach a camera company with your evidence
(If)–3   If you can set up a special deal
(A)–4   Approach a bank with your evidence and your deal.

It is likely that approaching a bank at this stage is going to be more successful than doing so at the outset when there is only an idea in your mind.

As I mention in my book *Opportunities*, the if-box map is always the best case scenario. You lay out what would happen if everything goes as you hope. There are no branch points. If you want to allow for alternative responses you simply create another if-box map.

Planning

In a fast-moving world plans are almost always wrong because they have to be based on the present state and the extrapolation of present trends. This fallibility of plans is not a reason to ignore them but a warning that they should not be made inflexible. One should plan to be in a position to change just as much as one should plan to be in a certain position. Planning for flexibility and uncertainty is important.

A plan can be regarded as a 'main stream' in which certain things are going to be done at certain times. Into this main stream feed the 'feeder-streams' of things that have to be done because they are essential for the main stream to move forward. This is shown in the figure below.

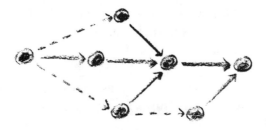

Of course, there may be points on the main stream where something has to be done in order to get the feeder stream moving. This is suggested by the broken lines. In the end one has something very like the well-established planning methods that are in use in business.

The design of a plan needs to include the change possibilities mentioned above. There should be flexibility so that the plan can still proceed if circumstances change (for instance, an exchange rate alteration). There should be change points so that an assessment of the situation at that point may lead to a change in route or objectives. There should be monitoring points at which it is possible to assess what is happening. There should be achievement stages so that the progress of the plan can be appreciated. Finally there should be cut-off points at which the plan can be abandoned if things have gone wrong (either because it has been a bad plan or because of gross changes in circumstances). The most important point is that these things are built into the plan — they are not just ways of treating a plan.

The terrain

All action is going to take place in the future. We can look at the future as a landscape in which the action is going to be worked out. This landscape or terrain has certain features which may be essential for the action or may help or hinder it. We can look at some of these in turn.

People

There are people who are going to be involved in designing or accepting the action proposals. There is delegation, instruction and communication to be considered. People may help or hinder. They may be neutral or inert. They may sabotage, resist, oppose – or delay. The logic-bubbles of the people involved may have to be examined to understand their motivations. It may be a matter of selecting the right people for the action.

Risks

All courses of action involve risk because the future can never be perfectly known. There are unknowns in terms of areas which cannot be fully known (like the reaction of the market to a product – in spite of market research). The behaviour of governments and competitors can be guessed at but not fully known. Then there are unknown changes like inflation, currency rates and prices of raw materials. Technology breakthroughs are other unknowns. There are actual dangers like faults in the product line or safety problems. There are shortfalls inasmuch as the initial predictions are not fulfilled.

Constraints

There are legal constraints, regulatory constraints and constraints imposed by distribution systems. There may be constraints of time and constraints of price. The constraints may be constant or they may be changing. A product designed before standards were set might be obsolete or unsaleable when standards emerge (either set by the major producer or by agreement).

Resources

Resources provide the 'energy' and the means for the action. Resources include people, money, time, effort, motivation, technical know-how, goodwill, market position and many other ingredients.

Future

Finally, there needs to be some assessment of possible future scenarios. These should take into account political changes such as a change of government. They should also take into account competitive behaviour — either because competitors are responding to your action or because they have their own courses of action.

Business and daily life

Some of the matters mentioned in this section might seem to apply more directly to business than to everyday life. This is because 'action' is the fundamental idiom of business. Something is always happening. There are always plans, strategies and objectives. In daily life it is possible to drift along quite comfortably from day to day without formally setting objectives. For those who do want to act in a more purposeful manner it should not be difficult to extract from this section those elements which can be made to apply to daily life — for example, the simple AGO or the if-box map.

Deliberate thinking

In the BBC Television series the audience were invited at random from organisations and schools in the neighbourhood. On several occasions certain youngsters in the audience seemed to outshine the others in being able to think clearly and to the point and to offer ideas and suggestions. In each case it was later found that these youngsters had in fact (unknown to us) been doing the CoRT thinking lessons in their schools. There could be no better demonstration of the effect of training in deliberate thinking.

As this is the last section of this book I want to be as focused and as practical as possible. What can one do about developing thinking as a usable skill?

There are four important aspects. To develop thinking as a skill it should be deliberate, focused, confident and enjoyable.

Deliberate

A thinker should be able to turn on his thinking at will. A thinker should be able to direct his thinking to any subject or any aspect of a subject. This is not to suggest that in between this deliberate use of thinking he does without thinking. There are 'general aspects' of thinking which apply at all times and which I shall discuss later in this section. At this point I want to emphasise the importance of being in control of one's thinking, of being able to use it *at will*.

Focused

Untrained thinking is usually of the point-to-point variety, drifting along from idea to idea. There is a lot of waffle and a lot of ineffectiveness. Such thinkers can often only become focused when they are attacking some point in the thinking of others. To be focused in thinking is one of the hardest things to achieve. The mind loves to wander off along interesting alleys that open up. There is room for this in thinking, especially in the creative aspects, but this hopeful drifting should not become the dominant idiom. In untrained thinking some idea triggers an emotion which in turn determines the way something is looked at, and then thinking just follows this path without any genuine exploration of the subject.

The thinking tools mentioned at different places in this book and used in the CoRT thinking lessons provide a means for being focused in thinking. You can set out to do a deliberate PMI or OPV – and then do it. The first step is to determine to do it. The second step is to do it. It is like giving a definite instruction to oneself.

The focus in thinking can be as tight as you wish. You may focus on 'bicycles' in general or you may focus on 'the shape of a spoke in a bicycle wheel'. Just as you might set a very general question or a very specific question in ordinary language, so in thinking the focus may be either.

Confident

Thinking should be confident. Any skill is better if it is done with confidence – be it skiing or playing tennis. There is, however, a big difference between being confident and being arrogant. To be sure that you are right, to be sure that your thinking is better than anyone else's, to be sure that there can be no alternatives, are all aspects of arrogance. As I mentioned earlier, arrogance is the major sin of thinking – because it kills thinking. A confident thinker is not necessarily a brilliant thinker. Confidence has nothing to do with value. It is the way something is done. A confident driver in a small car can drive with confidence. He may drive rather slowly. He knows the limits of his skill and exercises it with confidence.

A confident thinker does not have to prove himself right and the other person wrong. He or she sees the thinking as an operating skill, not as ego-achievement. A confident thinker is willing to listen to others. He is willing to improve his thinking by acquiring a new idea or a new way of looking at things. A confident thinker is willing to set out to think about something. He or she is able to acknowledge that an answer has not been found.

A confident cook is able to make mistakes and to learn from them.

Enjoyable

If we only take medicine when we are ill then medicine is never likely to become enjoyable. If we only use thinking when we have insoluble problems then thinking is not likely to become an enjoyable skill. Enjoying thinking does not necessarily mean being interested in puzzles, games and brainteasers. As a matter of fact I am not particularly interested in these myself. It is more a matter of being able to think about different things: of having ideas, of working things out, of engaging in a 'thinking' type discussion. There are boring discussions in which each party is trying to put across a particular point of view. There are enjoyable discussions in which each party is exploring the subject – and at the end of such a discussion both parties have new ideas and stimulated thoughts.

Children really do enjoy thinking. One youngster in Venezuela, who had previously nearly always played truant from school, persuaded his parents not to go on holiday because he would miss his thinking lessons. Adults too, can enjoy thinking when their egos are not being threatened and when there is some formal structure which encourages them to think. To serve this purpose I am considering setting up 'Thinking Clubs' to provide a framework within which people can enjoy using the skill of thinking – and also use their thinking in an effective manner to tackle different tasks. I shall discuss this later in this section.

Self-image

This is the most important point of all. I mentioned it at the beginning of the book and I shall emphasise it again here. The self-image of 'I am intelligent' or 'I am not an egg-head' is a value image which has to be defended or maintained. In the first case thinking is merely a tool to show how smart you are. In the second case thinking is avoided because it *has* to be regarded as 'boring'. The self-image of 'I am a thinker' is a totally different self-image. It is not a 'value' image but an operating image. In tennis the skill of playing tennis can be improved by attention and practice. The player enjoys playing even though he is not the best player in the world or even on that court. So it is with the self-image of 'I am a thinker'. It means that I can *try* to think about things, that I enjoy thinking about things, that I am interested in developing more skill at thinking.

If all my work, including this book, achieved no more than cause a shift to the self-image of 'I am a thinker', I would be happy. The techniques, understandings and methods are of secondary importance to this.

Time discipline

We like to feel that thinking should be free and unfettered. The paradox is that a strict time discipline enhances not only the effectiveness of thinking but also the enjoyment. You might set yourself to think about something for 30 seconds, or one minute or five minutes. In the CoRT thinking lessons in schools it is an essential part of the method that only a short time (two to four minutes) is allowed for thinking about an item.

There are many reasons behind the use of this time discipline. In the first place it makes thinking more deliberate and more focused. The thinker switches on his thinking and operates it. The thinker focuses directly on the task. In time he becomes much better at thinking clearly about the matter. Even more important than this is the freedom that the strict time discipline gives. The time discipline takes the burden and stress out of thinking. Instead of having to go on thinking until you have solved the problem or got a wonderful answer you just have to think for two minutes. That is the 'task' you have to perform. You know that at the end of that two minutes you can stop thinking – whether you have any idea or not. In practice it is surprising how effective this time discipline is in removing the anguish of thinking. At first people are a bit worried that they have not turned up any wonderful idea in the short time. With practice they appreciate that this is not the purpose. The purpose is that for the allotted time they should have been using their thinking – whatever the result.

With practice, even thirty seconds of thinking is a great deal of time. After all, complicated dreams are supposed to take place within a few seconds of real time.

Harvesting

This is another very important point. If you feel that you have only achieved something with your thinking when you have proved someone else wrong, solved the puzzle, found an answer to the problem or created a brilliant idea, then you are probably not going to try thinking in the first place. Certainly you are not going to try it for just a few minutes. 'Harvesting' is the other side of the coin to 'time-discipline'. The word 'harvesting' is used in its normal agricultural sense: bringing in the crop of apples, wheat or whatever it may be. In this case it is thoughts or ideas. It is a matter of making oneself aware of what has been achieved, even in a very brief thinking session. Perhaps some point has become more clear? Perhaps some idea has been identified as a blocking idea? Perhaps there is an actual suggestion? Perhaps some alternatives have been spelled out? Perhaps some point has been identified as a problem area that needs further thinking attention?

Sensitive harvesting means being acutely aware of just what has been achieved. There will always be something that has been achieved. It is a matter of being aware of it. The comment 'I just keep going round in circles' is a considerable achievement: as an identification of a 'locked-in' situation.

As an exercise think of one or other of the following subjects for just 30 seconds, and at the end of that time write down what you think can be 'harvested' from your thinking: buses, paying taxes, manners, the weather, Christmas, a watch, rabbits.

The exercise here is directly a 'harvesting' one. Later in this section I shall write about setting thinking tasks.

Thinking about thinking

The skilled thinker can do two things:

1 He or she can think about the subject: perform the thinking task.
2 He or she can think about the *thinking* used in performing the thinking task.

Thinking about thinking is not a common habit but it is an important part of the skill of thinking. A golfer thinks about his strokes. A tennis player thinks about his backhand or his serve. This 'standing back' and being able to watch oneself in action – almost as an outside observer – is an important part of skill building. The thinker should certainly get into the habit of being able to look at his or her own thinking. He should be able to look back at the thinking he has used in performing a thinking task. He should be able to look at the thinking he is using at the moment. He should be able to look at the thinking he feels he is going to use.

The thinker should also be able to look at the thinking used by other people or used 'in general about a particular subject'. Looking at the thinking of others does not mean doing so with the aim of criticising it or attacking it. The intention is to watch what thinking is being applied. Just as a bird-watcher watches birds. The better one gets at it, the more the fascination grows.

In looking at thinking, the following areas of observation may come to mind: blockages; the recurrence of certain ideas; emotional points; possible difficulties in generating more alternatives; blank spots; other ways of looking at things; the likelihood of a conclusion; the identification of any sticking points; difficulties in getting going; finding a starting point, etc.

It is a useful exercise to write down a whole repertoire of these observations. It is only by stocking your mind with such concepts that it becomes possible to 'observe' thinking. For example, the concept of 'value-laden' words then allows you to search for and pick these out. Once you become conscious of the various uses of value-laden words, they do stand out more obviously.

The TEC framework

This is a very simple structure for focusing thinking and making of it a deliberate task. The TEC structure itself will be incorporated in a 'five-minute think', which I shall describe later in the section. For the moment TEC is going to be treated in a more general sense.

'T' stands for 'Target' and 'Task'

The 'target' is the precise focus of the thinking. If we were looking at shoes we might choose to focus upon the heel or shoe style in general or the need for different right and left shapes. As mentioned under 'focus' the target may be as general or as tight as you wish. Indeed a tight target may have been defined in a previous thinking session.

The 'Task' is the thinking task that is to be performed. It may be a matter of 'review' which involves looking at the way something is being done with an eye to improvement. It may be a matter of 'fault finding' and 'fault correction'. It may be a matter of 'problem solving'. It may also just be a matter of 'problem finding'. The task may be a creative exercise: 'how else could I perform the function of a heel?' or 'how could heels be made more useful?'.

Any of the thinking tools mentioned in this book (or in the CoRT lessons) can become the 'task'. You may set yourself the task of doing a C & S or an AGO.

It is important to define both the target and the task rather precisely.

'E' stands for 'Expand' and 'Explore'

This is the opening-up phase. We could use lateral thinking techniques like the random word or provocation. We could do a CAF and consider all factors. We could scan our experience. We could analyse the situation. We could try to abstract familiar patterns.

In this phase we are opening up the field, filling in the map, exploring the territory. A certain amount of wandering is permissible at this point. It is not unlike those essay questions in school: 'Write all you know about . . . .'

The expansion is positive and free-flowing. We are not trying to exercise judgement or find the best ideas at this stage. We are pulling in information and concepts. 'Richness' is all important.

'C' stands for 'Contract' and 'Conclude'

This is the narrowing down phase. We are now trying to make sense of what we have. We are trying to come to a definite conclusion. This may be a solution, a creative idea, an additional alternative or an opinion. We can now use design, shaping and judgement. The conclusion is the outcome of our thinking, not just a summary of it. What does it boil down to? What does it add up to? What is the outcome? What is the result? There are three levels at which the 'conclusion' can be set:

1   A specific answer, idea or opinion.

2   A full harvesting of all that has been achieved. Including for example a listing of ideas considered.

3   An objective look at the 'thinking' that has been used.

Even in the absence of anything at level (1) there should be an output at levels (2) and (3).

As a simple framework TEC can be applied at any point: focus, set task, open up, narrow down and conclude.

The 5-minute think

This is a formal framework and it should be carried out formally with strict time discipline.

The timing is as follows:
1 minute: Target and Task
2 minutes: Expand and Explore
2 minutes: Contract and Conclude

Five minutes seems a very short time – which it is if the thinking is of the waffle variety. For focused thinking, however, it is a surprisingly long time. At first, many groups run out of thinking before they run out of time.

The 5-minute think can be done by individuals on their own or by groups. A group should not be larger than four members, otherwise each member gets too little participation time.

As mentioned above, the time discipline must be adhered to. This is important because it is the only form of discipline and adhering to it also means adhering to the focus. For example, it often happens that the thinker or the thinking group decides upon a target and task before the first minute is up. There is then a temptation to rush ahead to the next stage. This is to be avoided. The reason behind the strict adherence to the time is that if a thinker feels he or she may not have enough time in the expand and explore section, there is a temptation to rush the first section in order to create more time. The result is that the first section – which is deceptively simple – does not get proper attention. So stay with the first section until the time is up.

A sample 5-minute think is shown below. In practice the ideas would be thought about rather than written. The subject area is the telephone.

Target and Task (1 minute)
o new design of telephone
o correct some faults
o additional functions to be added to telephone
o some new type of telephone service
o concentrate on some major defect
o perhaps interruption is one of these
o ways of coping with telephone interruption

So the task is to find ways of coping with telephone interruption.

Expand and Explore (2 minutes)
o Use telephone answering machines.
o The Japanese have an answering machine to answer normal callers but special callers have a secret number which allows them to get through to the person.
o Have a secretary who says you are at a meeting.

- In the USA there are 'voice mail' systems which are essentially one-way telephones through which someone leaves a message in your computer 'mail box'. You clear your mail box as often as you like and call back and leave a message in the other party's mail box. So the telephone is no longer regarded as a 'real time' system.
- Some sort of special ringing tone – or better still a light – which allows you to tell whether the call is urgent. But people would cheat and claim all calls are urgent – which indeed it may be to them but not to you. Could you perhaps 'see' for yourself whether or not the call is urgent? A small print-out on a piece of paper of who the caller was and what he wanted would be a help. It could be on paper or on a screen. I believe there is such a device already in existence for deaf people.
- If it were on paper you could just tear off the list of names, numbers and reasons for calling and then call back when you wished. More convenient and quicker to scan than voices on a tape. But everyone would need the teletypewriter type entry. It would be a sort of Telex.

Contract and Conclude (2 minutes)
- It would be nice means of having some way of telling who it was and what was wanted. A secretary probably can do this but it still means interruption and a lot of your time and hers.
- A visual read-out at the time would be better. If you were very busy you would not bother to read this until later. If you were less busy and the call was important you might want to pick up the phone there and then.
- You could, of course, always ask people to telex instead of phoning. The technology is not difficult and a write-out device probably already exists for deaf people.
- The major snag is that the sender would need a key pad. How could we get around this?
- Perhaps the sender could use the ordinary dial numbers on any phone by tapping in a special code. This would mean that any ordinary telephone could be used.

Conclusion: a write out device that could be attached to any phone and operated from another phone just by using the ordinary dialling numbers.

Overview of thinking: problem finding and problem solving
Focus on one particular problem. There are ways of overcoming this but these are not good enough. Imagining of an 'ideal solution' and then looking around to make this practical. Developing the idea, then focusing on a deficiency. Finding a way around that deficiency. Final result is a particular product idea which opens up a new phone function.

The above sample does arrive at a definite conclusion. In other cases this may not be so. At the end of the 5-minute think there may only be a feeling of the *difficulty* of the subject or the need to set a more specific target. If this seems to be the case then the Expand and Explore section can actually be used to identify and formulate an 'approach' to the matter or to define a 'problem' that can be tackled in another section. The important thing is that the output must be definite, but that there are a large number of alternative outputs. It is enough that something has been achieved. It is unrealistic to expect the whole problem to be solved in 5 minutes.

There should be no sense of rush. If there is, then the target has been pitched too widely. It is also possible to repeat a 5-minute think with the same target. I would, however, advise against doing this immediately because there is a temptation to turn a 5-minute think into a 30-minute think through a succession of sessions on the same subject. This destroys the whole point of the exercise.

Symbolic TEC

A symbolic representation of TEC is shown in the figure below. These symbols can also be used separately as instructions to oneself or to others 'to focus' or 'to open up' or 'to narrow down or contract'. They could, for example, be placed in the margin of a report.

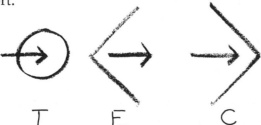

T   E   C

PISCO

A rather fuller framework is provided by PISCO. Both TEC and PISCO are more fully described in section VI of The CoRT Thinking Programme.

The letters in 'PISCO' stand for:

'P' stands for Purpose
What is the purpose of the thinking? What is expected as the end product? Why is the thinking being done? This is somewhat similar to the 'T' of TEC but with rather more emphasis on *why* the thinking is being done at all.

'I' stands for Input
This is the input of information, experience and all the ingredients that need to go into the thinking. At this stage the various tools such as CAF, C & S, OPV can be used to develop a rich map. This is somewhat similar to the 'E' part of TEC.

'S' stands for Solutions
These are alternative solutions, ideas or approaches to the matter. The word 'solution' suggests a problem, but in this case it merely indicates concrete alternatives which are offered. In this sense the 'S' is a narrowing down not unlike the 'C' of TEC.

'C' stands for Choice
This is the choice between the alternatives that have been offered at the previous stage. A decision and an evaluation is made at the end of which there is but one surviving alternative. The section on decision making could be of help here.

'O' stands for Operation
This is the action stage. This section is concerned with putting the chosen alternative into action. What are the steps to be taken? How is the matter to be staged? The implementation of the idea is focused upon at this point.

Symbolic PISCO

These are the symbols representing PISCO:

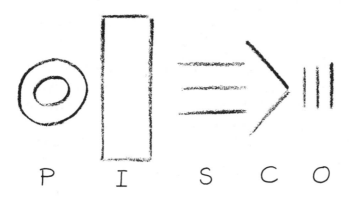

P I S C O

TEC–PISCO

The two frameworks can be combined. TEC is the more general framework. PISCO spreads out the stages and can be more useful if there is an actual problem or matter that has to be thought about. There is no particular time limit on the stages – just a consciousness of whichever stage is being used. At any point in the PISCO process an area that needs more thinking can be identified and the TEC frame can then be applied directly at that spot.

For general purposes and the exercise of thinking skill the TEC framework is sufficient and there is no need to go for the more elaborate PISCO.

Deliberate practice of thinking

We do not only learn to swim when we are drowning. Nor do we only learn swimming in order to avoid drowning. Swimming does serve this purpose but we also learn it to enjoy it. It could be the same with thinking. We could develop our thinking skill so that when we really need it, we will be both confident and fluent. We could also practice it because we actually enjoy applying our thinking to matters. Skiers ski because they enjoy skiing not just to develop a means of transport on snow. The exercise of skiing skill is a joy in itself. It can be the same with thinking but – as in skiing – there can be an awkward stage in which nothing much seems to be happening and little progress is made. In thinking this is the stage when thinking is still attached to the ego and the thinker wants to prove himself right and wants to solve all the problems of the world at every thinking session.

Someone who is not a bird-watcher cannot understand what a bird-watcher is doing. There seem to be some ordinary birds hopping about. There is always a need to build up some understanding of a field before the patterns start to emerge. It is at this point that the subject becomes fascinating. So it is with thinking. It is only after some practice and observation that it becomes fascinating.

Thinking Clubs

Thinking is already taught directly in several schools using the CoRT thinking lessons (published by Pergamon Press, Oxford). For those who have already left school – and for those who attend school where the lessons are not taught – there are no formal structures for the exercise of the general thinking skills that I have written about in this book. To provide such a structure I am proposing to set up 'thinking clubs' in which small groups of people can come together to exercise their thinking on specific subjects and to practise thinking skills in a deliberate and focused manner.

In a special section at the end of this book (*page 158*), I describe how to set up and run such a thinking club. I also give an address for those who may want more information about these clubs on *page 166*.

General thinking skills

In this section I have focused on the deliberate application of thinking to a particular situation at a particular time. The other aspect of thinking is when some of the habits, attitudes and strategies become 'second nature'. On the deliberate side one might sit down formally to do a 5-minute think. On the second nature side the thinking skills will be applied automatically in any situation without conscious effort. In the end one needs both: the general thinking skills as second nature and the ability to focus formally upon a matter. What does need saying, however, is that the formal stage is essential before the second nature stage develops.

In order to develop general thinking skills as second nature it is essential at some stage to have gone through the formal and deliberate practice of some of the processes. Otherwise these 'executive concepts' do not become part of thinking. Without such formal practice we are back to the old notion of good intentions: 'I am an intelligent person and I consider myself a thinking person – therefore there is nothing further that I need to do about it. I also consider myself open minded and willing to listen to others.' These vague intentions never do develop a person's thinking skill to its full capacity.

The sort of habits that might eventually become part of a person's general thinking skills might include the following.

An understanding of the importance of perception and the nature of perception as a pattern-making and pattern-using system.

An instinctive tendency to search for alternatives not only when there is a clear need for this, but also when there is no alternative in sight.

A dislike for arrogance in thinking.

A dislike of negative thinking and a preference for exlectics over dialectics. A disdain for negative thinking as one of the easier and cheaper forms of thinking.

A willingness to listen to the ideas of others. The habit of doing an OPV and examining logic-bubbles.

In an argument situation, the habit of doing both an EBS and an ADI. The ability to clarify values in such situations.

An overall view of the importance of emotions, feelings and values in thinking, but an effort to do some perceptual thinking before finally applying the emotions.

A broad scan of situations before coming to a conclusion. This might include things like the PMI, CAF and C & S.

The ability to make decisions.

The ability to set up objectives and sub-objectives and to design courses of action.

The ability to use ideas for their 'movement value' and also to set up and use deliberate provocation.

An understanding of lateral thinking and the willingness to change perceptions – even if this is not successful. The courage to use such techniques as the random word stimulation when ideas are needed.

The ability to switch into formal, focused thinking.

A liking for effectiveness. An appreciation of 'operacy'.

A clear appreciation of thinking as a skill and a self-image as a 'thinker'.

Summary

What I have written in this book is based on many years of experience in the teaching of thinking in a practical manner to different ages, abilities and cultures. It is only too easy to sit down in a corner and to analyse what thinking ought to be and then to propose this analysis as a way of teaching thinking. That can do – and does – great damage to the practical teaching of thinking.

One aspect of the teaching of thinking is the need to remove certain misconceptions and to undo certain habits. For example, we really do need to stop considering thinking as simply 'intelligence in action'. We do need to think of it as a *skill* that can be developed by everyone. We do need an awareness of the 'intelligence trap'. We do need to encourage the self-image of 'I am a thinker'.

We also need to appreciate the domination of Western thinking habits by the negative idiom: clash, criticism and dialectics. We need to put negative thinking in its proper place as part of thinking. We need to put creative, constructive and design thinking before negative thinking.

We need to change our conceptions about thinking and action. To effect this change we need a concept such as 'operacy' which gives status to the thinking involved in doing. We need to appreciate effectiveness and not just intellectual games.

We need to understand the major role of perception in thinking. We need to understand how perception works as a self-organising patterning system with all that follows. For example, lateral thinking then follows directly and logically.

We need to place emotions, feelings and values in their proper perspective. In the end they are the most important part of thinking – but only if they are used in the end rather than at the beginning.

We need to understand the practical value of being formal and deliberate about thinking instead of just waffling about. In the end we may prefer the habits, attitudes and strategies to become second nature but they will not become that just by our wishing it to be so. The formal and deliberate stages have to come first.

So a certain amount of this book has been devoted to these matters of understanding, appreciation, putting things in perspective, undoing misconceptions and attempting to trigger insights into thinking. At times the case may have been overstated and put too harshly, but my experience in the field has suggested the necessity for this. The biggest enemy of thinking is the feeling 'that our thinking is pretty good anyway and we do not need to do anything about it'. I do not subscribe to this view. I think we have done well in technical matters and appallingly elsewhere. I believe we would have progressed much faster if we had been less complacent about our thinking skills and less inclined to delegate thinking to those who were using an antiquated idiom.

At times it has been necessary to create new words to focus better upon a concept. For example – it was necessary to invent the term 'lateral thinking' many years ago in order to focus upon an area which overlaps with creativity but is quite distinct. The word 'po' is another such necessary invention, which arises directly from the logic of patterning systems. In this book I have introduced other concepts such as 'movement value' (of an idea); 'exlectics' (as distinct from dialectics); 'logic-bubble' (to describe in a direct way the complex of perceptions and structure within which another person acts logically); 'operacy' (as distinct from description-type thinking). These are all offered as serious and necessary concepts. I believe they ought to be part of the language because without new words we cannot 'hold' new concepts – they just drift off into the old concepts if we have to use the old words.

Then there are descriptive phrases like 'intelligence trap'; 'Everest effect'; 'Village Venus effect'; 'shooting questions and fishing questions'; 'dense reading'; 'decision pre-frame and post-frame'. These have only a descriptive or communication value. Those that are convenient may survive and those that are unnecessary will disappear. It is enough that they will have served to communicate an idea.

Finally we come to the specific tools – 'the attention-directing techniques'. Those who wish to understand the full purpose behind these may want to read my book *Teaching Thinking*. I am well aware that a mass of initials such as PMI, CAF, C & S, AGO, OPV, HV and LV seem highly artificial and unnecessary. Indeed this is exactly what the teachers complained about when I first introduced the initials in the CoRT thinking lessons. This was before the lessons had been used. After some experience the teachers came back and asked for more such 'shorthand devices'. They had found that in practice there is a need for a strange, simple instruction that one can give to one's own thinking or the thinking of others. Whether we like it or not, the instruction 'do a PMI' is more powerful than exhortation to look always at both sides of the matter. This is not surprising because that is how patterning systems work.

These tools (PMI etc) can be practised deliberately and the practiser feels that he is making progress in mastering that particular tool. The operation then enters his repertoire of concepts as an 'executive concept' – in other words he learns action concepts not just description concepts.

As the reader may well imagine I have, over the years, lived through endless attacks about jargon and artificiality. These are made by people with no practical experience of teaching thinking and who find it easier to fasten on to this point than to discuss the basic concepts. In the end practicality must win. Experience with the teaching of thinking to thousands of adults and youngsters supports the use of these 'attention handles'. As a matter of fact I, myself, dislike jargon and that is why I avoid the usual psychological jargon since I am not writing for psychologists.

There are people who feel that if they pay close attention to their thinking then they will become self-conscious about it and become like the centipede that was immobilised by self-consciousness about which leg preceded which. This is a valid point and there are some elaborate schemes for thinking that do have this effect. Readers will have noticed, however, that the tools suggested in this book are no more than 'attention-directing' tools. There is no elaborate and confusing scheme as to which step follows which. You do your thinking as you have always done, but you may insert, at different times and in any order, such attention directors as PMI or OPV in order to make things more clear. If you were to forget everything except one technique (for example, the PMI) you would still have gained something. In an elaborate scheme if you forget part of it you are not only confused but also lost.

Must one really practise thinking in the deliberate manner suggested in this book? The answer is yes. There are insights, understandings and awarenesses that will improve your thinking just as you read about them. For example, your attitude to negative thinking might change. But there are other aspects which do require *deliberate* practice. For instance, everyone has the general intention of considering other people – but deliberately to practice an OPV gives a very different result. You can read any amount you like about cooking or golf or driving a car but in the end it is practice that matters.

Those who have always thought that their own thinking has always been pretty wonderful, will probably continue to do so and may find this book unnecessary. Good luck to them. I always remember when my first books on lateral thinking were published. I had letters from some of the most creative people in the world who had found the books to be of value to them.

I would end with a summary of my experience. If you have seen young people given permission to think then you have seen a vision.

Reference
material

Books by Edward de Bono

The use of lateral thinking Cape, 1967; Penguin Books, 1971.
Published as *New think: the use of lateral thinking in the generation
of new ideas* New York: Basic Books, 1968.

The five-day course in thinking New York: Basic Books 1967; Allen
Lane, 1968; Penguin Books, 1969 with a card 'The L game' as insert.

The mechanism of mind Cape, 1969; Penguin Books, 1971; New
York: Simon and Schuster, 1969.

Lateral thinking: a textbook of creativity Ward Lock, 1970;
Penguin Books, 1977. Also published as *Lateral thinking: creativity
step by step* New York: Harper, 1973.

Lateral thinking for management McGraw-Hill, 1971; Penguin
Books, 1982; New York: American Management Association, 1971.

Technology today Routledge and Kegan Paul, 1971; Penguin Books,
1982.

*Practical thinking: four ways to be right, five ways to be wrong, five
ways to understand* Cape, 1971; Penguin Books, 1976.

The dog-exercising machine Cape, 1971; Penguin Books, 1971; New
York: Simon and Schuster, 1971.

Children solve problems Allen Lane, 1972; Penguin Books, 1972;
New York: Harper, 1974.

Po: beyond yes and no Penguin Books, 1972. Also published as
PO: a device for successful thinking New York: Simon and Schuster,
1972.

* These books are referred to in the text.

Think tank Think Tank Corporation, Canada, 1973.

Eureka! an illustrated history of inventions from the wheel to the computer Thames and Hudson, 1974; paperback 1979; New York: Holt, 1974; Harper, Row and Winston, 1979.

*Teaching thinking M. Temple Smith, 1976; Penguin Books, 1979; New York: Transatlantic, 1977.

The greatest thinkers: the thirty minds that shaped our civilization Weidenfeld and Nicolson, 1976; New York: Putnam, 1976.

Word power: an illustrated dictionary of vital words Pierrot Publishing, 1977; Penguin Books, 1979; New York: Harper and Row, 1977.

The happiness purpose M. Temple Smith, 1977; Penguin Books, 1979.

The case of the disappearing elephant: a 3G mystery Dent, 1977.

*Opportunities: a handbook of business opportunity search Associated Business Programmes, 1978; Penguin Books, 1980.

Future positive M. Temple Smith, 1979; New York: Transatlantic, 1980.

Atlas of management thinking M. Temple Smith, 1982.

*These books are referred to in the text.

Thinking Lessons

CoRT Thinking Lessons, published by Pergamon Press, Headington Hill Hall, Oxford.

L-Game:

This is now manufactured by de Bono Products Ltd.
Mountbatten House, Victoria Street, Windsor, Berkshire
(note: this game is protected by copyright and patent 1148172)

Other matters:

For information on Thinking Clubs, courses in thinking, seminars, industrial training, the newsletter to thinkers, Think-Links and Junior Course in Thinking, write to:
Edward de Bono PO Box 3 DB London WIA 3DB

How to set up a thinking club

There are tennis courts for tennis, golf courses for golf and ski slopes for skiing. If thinking really is a skill where do we get to practise it? There are puzzles, crossword puzzles, detective stories and board games but these only cover a tiny part of thinking. Many people who are good thinkers and who enjoy thinking do not like solving puzzles or playing games – they prefer thinking that is broad and effective and has more to do with wisdom than with cleverness. We are forced to use our thinking when there is a major decision to be made – for example, when buying a house or changing a job. It would not be much good if we only practised swimming when we were about to drown. Thinking only when we are forced to, provides neither practice nor enjoyment. Thinking becomes like medicine: something we only use when we are in trouble.

A thinking club is a place for the practice and enjoyment of thinking as a skill. There are no right answers to be reached and no tests. A thinking club is for those who want to enjoy thinking and for those who want to develop their skill at thinking. Thinking is no different from any other skill or hobby – if you want to get enjoyment from it you need to put in some effort. Walking along the road will not make you a better tennis player or a better skier. You need deliberate practice in a place that is set up for such practice.

Qualifications

To set up or to join a thinking club there is only one qualification. That single qualification is motivation. You have got to be interested in thinking and you have got to want to do something about it.

There are many organisations which you cannot join unless you have the right degree or certificate or IQ level. This is not the case with the thinking clubs. Anyone may join if he or she is sufficiently motivated. In fact this makes things rather more difficult since genuine motivation is rare.

There are many people who say they are interested in thinking in a general sort of way but are not prepared to do very much about it. Motivation can be tested in two very practical ways. The first way is the 'cash-value' of that interest. Would you be prepared to spend the price of a cigarette every week on that activity? What about the price of a pack of cigarettes? What about the price of a meal out or an evening's entertainment? Any person can test his own motivation in that way.

The second test of motivation is to assess the 'priority-value' of an interest. Does that interest take precedence over other things? Would you make a point of going to a thinking club meeting on a regular basis, or only if there was nothing better to do that evening? At this point it is easy to see that although motivation is a qualification that is open to everyone, it is a rather difficult qualification.

The purpose of the thinking club is to provide a time and a place for the enjoyment and practice of thinking. The formality of the occasion is the main advantage. Everyone knows what they are there for — otherwise they should not be there.

Type of thinking

The type of thinking to be used in the thinking clubs is very much the type of thinking that I have outlined in this book. It has the following features.

It is concerned with wisdom more than with cleverness. The flavour is more that of robust commonsense rather than intellectual nit-picking.

Effectiveness is an important aspect, and this is reflected in the concept of 'operacy' which involves the thinking that is required to get things done. It is the opposite of ineffectual thinking.

It is definitely *not* the type of thinking used to prove yourself right and the other person wrong. The thinking club is not a place for argument and prejudice and defending your point of view. It is a place for open exploration of a subject and honest assessment. The thinking club is for people who want to use thinking in an exploratory way — not for those who want a place to show how right they are or how bright they are. This point will need emphasising from time to time.

The emphasis is on perception — on how we look at things. It is not on complicated processing in the form of mathematics or other procedures.

The thinking is to be neutral and objective. The thinking clubs are not there to promote any political or religious point of view.

The thinking is to be positive and constructive. The negative has a place in thinking, but it is an inferior place to the positive and the constructive. In the thinking clubs, proving other people to be foolish does not have the high esteem it may carry elsewhere.

Humour should play an important role. There is no reason at all why thinking should be solemn and humourless. Even if a serious subject is being discussed the thinking need not be heavy.

Clarity and simplicity are important. Thoughts should be expressed in as clear a manner as possible. Being complicated for the sake of being complicated is to be condemned.

Arrogance is the major sin.

Above all the thinking clubs are there for the exercise and enjoyment of the skill of thinking. This means looking at that skill objectively and detaching it from one's ego.

Throughout there are two types of thinking. Firstly, there is the thinking about the subject itself. Secondly, there is the thinking about *how* we are thinking about the subject (values, prejudices, getting blocked, lack of ideas etc). This ability to look at one's thinking is exactly like the ability of a golfer or skier to look at how he is performing in order to improve his skill.

Activities

The purpose of the thinking clubs is to provide a place, time and framework for the enjoyment, practice, development and application of thinking skills. There are three stages.

1   Learning basic thinking skills.
2   Practice of these skills.
3   Application of these skills.

At first much of the activity of the clubs will be concerned with learning the basic skills so that they can be used fluently and deliberately. It is a mistake to assume that thinking will be learned just because a subject is being thought about and discussed. There needs to be a direct focus of attention on the skills as such. Later on, when the skills have been developed, thinking can be applied in a practical fashion to specific problems and tasks. These may be current issues, personal problems, design of businesses and many other activities. A particular book, article or television programme might become the subject of focused thinking. A member of the club may bring a personal or business problem to the meeting. The thinking may be directed to planning and carrying out a certain task (bearing in mind that 'effectiveness' is a very important part of the type of thinking in use in the clubs). All these are later stages and it is a mistake to try to feed them in at too early a stage.

Formality and discipline

It may come as a shock to readers to find that I put the highest value on formality and discipline in the thinking clubs. Because I am in favour of free-ranging, exploratory thinking and breaking out of rigid tracks, it might seem that I would avoid formality and rigid structures. In fact the opposite is the case. Since there are no right answers and no fixed ideas there has to be a very strong discipline of structure. Without such a structure there would be drift, waffle and mess. Just as in training for ballet dancing or for sport the benefit of discipline is that it gets things done. If thinking is a skill that is to be used in a focused and deliberate manner then we must be able to direct it at will. It is the very rigidity of structure that gives the freedom of content.

Time discipline is important. If a meeting is to last one hour then it should last exactly one hour. If a problem is to be thought about for three minutes then at the end of that three minutes a bell is rung and the thinking ceases. As I mentioned elsewhere in this book this sort of time discipline is actually liberating. It means that one can focus exactly on an issue. It means that thinking is being performed for a finite time – not until the problem has been solved.

Discipline and ritual are a good substitute for enthusiasm, as is well known in any monastery. Enthusiasm comes and goes and depends on the mood of the moment. Discipline keeps things going when the initial enthusiasm wanes and until a different sort of enthusiasm takes over. In addition, a formal discipline means that thinking can be directed at the subject matter instead of at the structure itself.

I hope I have made this point forcefully enough. Long experience has shown that it is extremely important in the development of thinking skills. Without it I do not believe the thinking clubs will work. For example, the meeting times need to be set in a formal manner well in advance (for instance the first and third Monday of each month), otherwise it becomes impossible to please everyone and the sense of commitment is lost.

Organisation

There are many aspects of organisation: people, meeting place, timing, agenda, communication etc.

People

A thinking club consists of exactly six people. These are the members. There may be a small number of associates who attend the meetings but are not full members. If one of the full members does not attend the meetings on a regular basis then his place is taken by an associate (a member should attend at least three-quarters of the meetings). When there are enough associates a separate thinking club of six can form. There may be temporary states – for example, when the club is starting – when there are fewer than six members. The number six is chosen because it is best for the practice of thinking skills. The six can work as a group of six or split into two groups of three.

Organiser and host: The organiser has overall responsibility for the meeting and acts as host as well. It is up to the organiser to see that the meeting takes place and to control what happens during the meeting. The organiser should be an effective and competent person who is also good at getting on with people. Someone with charm but no competence is not much good for this role. The organiser may delegate the following roles: time-keeper, note-taker and communicator. The same organiser should continue throughout the life of the club. It is best not to rotate this position. If another member really wants to become the organiser – and shows enough competence – then there could be a change of organiser on a six monthly basis. But the role should not be rotated amongst other members who are neither willing nor capable of doing it. There should always be a back-up organiser in case the organiser is ill or unable to attend a meeting.

Time-keeper: This is an important role because the time-keeper has to be accurate and ruthless. The meetings must start on time and end exactly on time – even if that means stopping in the middle of something interesting. The time-keeper also keeps the time for each practice item. Many digital watches have stop watch functions. Sloppiness in time-keeping soon leads to general sloppiness and lack of focus.

Note-taker: The note-taker's task is to produce a summary report of each meeting for the log-book. There is a great deal of skill involved in putting things succinctly and yet in a way which captures the essence of what has been said. The summary should be between three and five hundred words.

Communicator: It is the role of the communicator to remind members of the next meeting and to be sure they let him know in good time if they are unable to attend.

Meeting place

The ideal meeting place is a home. A pub lacks the necessary formality. The meeting place should always be at the same place and the meeting held at the same time. It is not a good idea to rotate the meeting place. A back-up place should be considered in case the main place is not available on any occasion.

Frequency

The best frequency is once a fortnight. Once a week is too often and once a month too infrequent. The dates should be fixed in advance and should be on a predictable basis (for example the first and third Monday in each month). Trying to arrange dates to suit everyone is an impossibility. Allowances will need to be made for holiday seasons.

Duration

The first four meetings should not last longer than one hour each. The next four should last one and a half hours. After that the meetings can last two hours. At the end of the set time the meeting should be terminated even if the members linger on for social reasons. It is often a temptation to continue with the thinking and discussion if these are going well. That is a mistake to be avoided because it shifts the emphasis from the exercise of thinking skills to 'finding solutions' and changes the nature of the meetings.

Log-book

Each thinking club should have a log-book which carries a report on each meeting. This would give the time, place and people present. It would also give the 'agenda' and a summary of the thinking that took place.

Registration

I intend to set up a register of thinking clubs and also to establish a communication medium for them. An address for communication is given at the end of this section.

Content

In order to provide some uniform base-line of attitudes towards thinking, it is assumed that all members of the thinking club will have read a copy of this book. This makes it possible to refer to the various processes used in this book without having to explain them all again in detail.

Agendas for two trial meetings are provided here. Agendas for subsequent meetings can be obtained by writing to me at the address given at the end of the section.

Two things are important as regards the content of the meetings. The first thing is that at the beginning the emphasis needs to be directly and exclusively on practice and development of the basic thinking skills. There is a great temptation to try to do too much at first. This usually results in an argument type of discussion and a certain pointlessness which destroy the idiom of the meetings. The second thing is the need – always – to keep a balance between serious subjects and fun subjects. People tend to expect thinking to be 'serious' and 'heavy' but that is also a mistake. Far better practice is obtained on remote or fun subjects than on serious subjects, for on the serious subjects people just trot out their prejudices and stereotypes instead of thinking. Confidence in thinking needs to be built up on other matters first. The ratio between fun and serious subjects should be at least equal and preferably three to one in favour of the fun subjects (at least at first).

Trial meeting 1

A sample agenda for this meeting follows.

1 The organiser explains that the subject of the meeting is to be the focus skill PMI. He reminds the members of the nature of PMI, looking in the 'Plus' direction, then the 'Minus' direction and finally the 'Interesting' direction. *time 2–3 minutes*

2 **First practice:** the group of six works as a whole group together. Two minutes for plus points, two minutes for minus points and two minutes for interesting points. The time-keeper keeps this timing exactly.
Subject: 'Everyone should wear a badge showing his or her mood'.
time 6 minutes
(Note that when the group works as a whole no feedback time is required.)

3 **Second practice:** two groups of three are set up. The two groups should move somewhat apart so that separate discussions are taking place. Each group works through the PMI, spending two minutes on each section. The time-keeper keeps the exact time for both groups and tells them when to move on to the next part. At the end of the six minutes the groups meet together again and each group reports its output. This is the 'feedback' part. Someone in each group should have kept simple notes.
Subject: 'It would be useful to have eyes in the back of our heads, as well as the usual ones.'
working time 6 minutes, feedback time 4 minutes, total 10 minutes.

4 **Third practice:** each individual is assigned to do just one section (P or M or I). Individuals work alone for 2 minutes.
Subject: 'Instead of barking, watchdogs should be trained to go and quietly press a burglar alarm button.'

At the end of two minutes the group reassembles and each person in turn gives the feedback.
working time 2 minutes, feedback time 4 minutes.

5 **Fourth practice:** two groups of three with each group going through the entire PMI process. Two minutes on each section with change over signalled by the time-keeper. At the end of six minutes the groups meet to report and compare their thoughts.
Subject: 'On leaving school every youngster should spend a year doing "national service" which would consist of community service, hospital work, teaching etc.'
working time 6 minutes, feedback time 5 minutes, total 11 minutes.

6 **Discussion section:** This would cover such points as the following:
The value of doing a PMI.
When would a PMI be most useful?
The dangers of doing a PMI.
Whether the formality of the PMI seems strange at first.
Whether the strict, and short, time seems awkward at first.
The difficulty of the 'Interesting' part of the PMI.
Points for discussion could also be taken from the relevant section of this book.
total time 10 minutes.

7 **Fifth practice:** The group works as a whole. Two minutes in rotation are spent on each of the sections monitored as usual by the time-keeper.
Subject: 'At elections everyone should have two votes and one of these can be used negatively to cancel a vote for a disliked candidate'.
time 6 minutes.

8 **Practice items:** Each individual spends three minutes noting down 'practice items' which could be used on future occasions for the application of thinking skills. These should be of both the 'fun' and 'serious' types. Each individual offers his items and the note-taker collects them to start a stockpile of such items.
working time 3 minutes, feedback time 4 minutes, total time 7 minutes.

9 **End of session:** Reminder of next section and thinking skill which is to be the APC. Members to read relevant section of this book.
time 1 minute.

Total time 60 minutes
The overall timing of 60 minutes should be kept to. If necessary the working time on each section can be reduced (even to one minute for a practice item). The session devoted to inventing new practice items can be shortened or even omitted if necessary. What is important is that the overall time discipline be kept. Otherwise the sessions expand into long waffle sessions.

Once the session is over the club members may want to linger on for social reasons but there should be no further direct exercise of the thinking skills or discussion of them. Later on each session will extend for two hours, but this is too much at the beginning.

Trial meeting 2

A sample agenda for this meeting follows.

1   The organiser explains that the subject of the meeting is to be the focus skill APC, which stands for Alternatives, Possibilities and Choices.
The emphasis is on generating alternatives – alternative ways of looking at things, alternative ways of doing things.
time for this explanation 2–3 minutes.

2   **First practice:** Each individual works on his or her own to offer alternative explanations for what is described under the 'subject' heading. Time allowed is two minutes. At the end of that time the individuals come together to compare their explanations.
Subject: 'Early one morning a woman is seen to be burying three red socks in the garden, each sock in a separate hole. What alternative explanations could there be ?'
working time 2 minutes, feedback time 4 minutes, total 6 minutes.

3   **Second practice:** the group splits into three pairs. Each pair works for three minutes to generate as many approaches as possible for the given task. At the end of the time the pairs come together to compare notes.
Subject: 'Find different ways of measuring the total amount of fluid which a person drinks in twenty-four hours.'
working time 3 minutes, feedback time 4 minutes, total 7 minutes.

4   **Third practice:** the group sit together. The organiser goes round the circle asking each individual in turn for an alternative. If an individual cannot find a further alternative then he or she 'passes' and it becomes the next person's turn. When more than three people pass one after the other it is thrown open to further alternatives from anyone in the group.
Subject: 'Find alternative ways of saving energy either in the house or in general. This refers to the sort of energy that has to be paid for.'
time allowed: up to 8 minutes, then a cut-off.

5   **Fourth practice:** two groups of three work to suggest alternative courses of action in the given situation. At the end of three minutes the, groups compare their alternatives.
Subject: 'A father finds that his eighteen-year-old son has taken the family car and sold it to pay some desperate debts. The son reveals who has bought the car. What alternative courses of action are open to the father?'
working time of 3 minutes, feedback time of 4 minutes, total 7 minutes.

6   **Discussion section:** This would cover points raised in the relevant section of this book and also points such as the following:
When do we look for alternatives and when do we not?
What are the dangers in always looking for alternatives?
Why is it sometimes difficult to find alternatives?
Should all alternatives be listed, even the unlikely ones?
How broadly should alternatives be grouped?
Are the alternatives all in the same direction or each in a different direction?
total time of 10 minutes with sharp cut-off.

7   **Fifth practice:** the group works as a whole. Two minutes, individual thinking time is given first. Then the organiser goes around the group getting from each member an alternative for each of the items given

in the subject list. That alternative must perform the same function.
Subject: 'Alternatives that could perform same function as ladder, cup, dog, key, window'
individual thinking time 2 minutes, feedback 4 minutes, total 6 minutes.

8 **Sixth practice:** the group works as a whole to come up with alternative approaches to the problem given. These approaches are then sorted into some broad groupings.
Subject: 'Alternative approaches to the problem of the increase in street crime. Note that an approach does not mean finding a solution but includes ways of tackling or looking at the problem.'
time 7 minutes.

9 **Practice items.** Each individual spends two minutes designing a 'practice item' which could be used in a similar session on the APC focus skill. These should be of both the 'fun' and the 'serious' type. These are discussed and the note-taker collects them for the stockpile.
thinking time 2 minutes, feedback time 2 minutes

10 **End of session.** Notice of time and subject of next session.

As before, the overall timing should be adhered to even if this means shortening the time allowed for each item. In particular feedback time should not be allowed to over-run. The practice item generation at the end can be dropped if there is insufficient time.

Things to avoid

Experience has shown that the following things tend to wreck thinking club sessions – even though these things at first seem attractive.

Lack of time discipline and an over-running of a discussion that has become 'interesting'.

Lack of focus on the specific thinking skill that is being practised at the moment. The result is general waffle and discussion.

Ego type argument and the need to prove a point, prove yourself right, prove the other party wrong.

Tackling too many solemn or 'heavy' subjects and getting bogged down in stereotypes and parades of facts.

Inability to see that simple processes practised on 'fun' items do build up to a powerful skill.

Too much ambition and too much hurry to apply the developing thinking skills to 'real matters' or to solving the personal problems of members. In time this is an aim of the clubs but not for quite a while.

General sloppiness and the feeling that structure does not matter.

Getting too bogged down in the subjects rather than regarding them as practice items.

Being unwilling to look at the 'thinking' involved and not just at the subject.

A feeble organiser, or attempts to rotate the functions with the result that a feeble organiser is reached.

Lack of humour.

Political or ideological bias.

All these things can be avoided through a rigorous attention to focus, structure and time discipline. Waffle, ego and arrogance are the great enemies. Motivation is important. If a member is not sufficiently motivated to attend the meetings, throw him or her out.

Thinking club members

Where do the members come from? Someone who has read this book can invite his or her friends over for a meal or a drink to discuss the idea. Get the other people to read the book first or at least this section on thinking clubs. Put up a notice in the library or place of work and get people to contact you. Put a notice in the local paper asking people in the neighbourhood to contact you. People who are members of one group may also want to form a group of their own. In that case prospective members can be taken as guests to the existing club's meetings.

Discuss the BBC television series and/or any of my books and mention the idea of setting up a thinking club. Discuss the teaching of thinking at school and regard the club as a way of doing this with people who are no longer at school.

A family may form a thinking club on its own – or with a neighbouring family. Set up a group for neighbourhood children.

Thinking clubs do provide a formal reason for people to meet each other on a regular basis without the costs of the usual entertainment required on such occasions. As a starter, however, it may be worth inviting a few 'likely' friends to a party of which one hour could be devoted to the trial agenda given in this section. If the tone is kept definite and focused but not threatening or boring then most people enjoy using their minds in this way. People enjoy having a framework within which to meet and talk to other people.

Registration and further information:

This section on thinking clubs is quite brief since it forms part of another book. Those who want further information should send me a stamped self-addressed envelope of a reasonable size. It is also my intention to set up a register of thinking clubs (and thinkers) and to provide other material such as agendas for each meeting and, later on, thinking tasks. The only qualification is motivation. That seems much easier than it really is.

For further information write to Thinking Information P.O. Box 3DB London W1A 3DB

Index

abstraction 51
action and thinking 15, 123
ADI 89
AGO 126
alternatives 26
– in decisions 110
analysis 52
APC 27, 33
arrogance 16, 136
art 53
attention directing tools
   15, 136, 141

back-up thinking 12, 18

CAF 74
clash system 56, 71, 84,
   85, 86, 87, 97
classification 52
cleverness 3, 13, 15, 76
clubs, thinking 137, 149
communication 98
complexity contents
conclusion 143
confidence 136
CoRT lessons
   13, 19, 21, 135, 153
– methodology 13, 24
course of action 36
critical intelligence 12
criticism, destructive 86
– negative 86
C & S 75
cut-off 38

Darwin 31
de Bono's 2nd law 31
– Balaam's ass 113
– best home 116
– dice method 111
– easy way out 112
– spell-out 113
– ideal solution 115
– what if? 116
– simple matrix 118
– full matrix 119
– laziness 120
decisions 36, 109
– alternatives 111
– emotions 110
– fall-back 121
– implementation 121
– information 110
– post-frame 120
– pre-frame 110
– terrain 121
deliberate thinking 135
dense reading and
   listening 77
design 35
– alternatives 37
– constructive 96
– freezing 38
dialectics 97

EBS 88
education fallacies 10
education and
   intelligence 10
educators 10
effective thinker 15
emotions 99
– and decisions 109
enjoyment of
   thinking 15, 137
escape method 66
Everest effect 12

executive concept
   34, 149, 153
exlectics 88
experience scan 21, 74
experiments 81
– boards 31
– eggs 126
– orange juice
fall-back position 121
feelings 99, 100, 103
– changing 103
FI–FO 82
five-minute think 142
focus 135
– time discipline 138
forecasting 36

general thinking skills 148
grouping 52
gut-feeling 99

harvesting 139
hindsight 58
humour 57
HV and LV 104
hypothesis 32, 34, 82

if-box maps 130
information and
   thinking 17, 72
– decisions 109
– gaps 83
– negative 82
– selecting 82
– self-organising 53, 57, 59
– systems, active and
   passive 46
intelligence 9
– critical 12
– education 10
– genes 10
– waste of brilliant minds 12
intelligence trap
   11, 87, 100, 151

judgement 61

Lamarck 32
lateral thinking 55, 59
– and creativity 59
– as process 60
L-Game origin 29
logic 72
logic-bubbles 91, 92, 133

maps 88, 93, 121
– if-box 130
– gelatine 47
– towel 46
– trays 46
motivation 93
movement 62
movement value
   23, 62, 63, 64, 65

negotiating 89, 97

objectives 126
– setting 126
– sub 126

observing thinking skills
   10, 140, 141, 143
operacy 73, 124
OPV 93

patterns 56
– asymmetric 58
– centring 46
– changing 56
– making 26, 39, 45
– mistakes 50
– switching 58
– using 26, 39, 49
perception 35, 39
– and feeling 99, 101
– logic-bubbles 91, 92
– and processing 39
PISCO 146
planning 132
PMI 18
po 63
point-to-point thinking
   70, 132
practising thinking skills
   10, 25, 147
progress 55
provocation 61, 63, 64, 65

questions
– fishing 80
– shooting 80

random stimulation
   method 68
recognition 49, 50
– mistakes 50
reversal, in provocation 65
risks 133

scan, experience 21, 74
science 31, 32, 52, 53
science fiction 37
self-image 16, 137, 150, 151
skill of thinking 9
slow thinking 17
Socratic dialogue 86
spectacles method 21
stepping-stone method 64
strategy 128

tactics 128
targets 127, 141
task 141
teaching thinking 13, 14, 99,
   100
– experience 151
– Schools Council 14
– transfer 14
– Venezuela 13
TEC 141
– decisions 121
– plans 133
thinker, effective 15
– definition 15
thinking, as a skill 9, 11
– definition 11
– deliberate 135
– and doing 123
– focus 135
– general skills 148
– reactive and projective 12
– and violence 100
thinking about thinking 140
thought experiment 81
time-discipline 138
– five-minute think 142
– focus 135
tool method 15, 136, 141

value-laden words 106
values 97, 99, 104
– 4M 104
– HV and LV 104
variable value 97
Venezuela 13, 14
verbal fluency 12
village Venus effect 31
violence and thinking 100

wisdom 13, 15, 76
working backwards 129